SELECTED POEMS

1977–2005

Other books by Celestine Frost

An Inhuman Rival
New Rivers Press, 1977

The Choice
Spectacular Diseases, 1990

An Imagined Experience over the Entrance
Dusty Dog, 1992

I Gathered My Ear from the Green Field
Logodaedalus, 1996

A Yelp in the Ideal
Codhill Press, 2002

Great Poems for Grand Children
Editor
AARP/Sterling, 2010

SELECTED POEMS

1977 – 2005

Celestine Frost

CODHILL

Codhill Press books
are published for David Appelbaum

First edition
Printed in the United States of America

Library of Congress Cataloging-in-Publication Data
Frost, Celestine.
[Poems. Selections]
Selected poems 1977-2005 / Celestine Frost. -- 1st ed.
p. cm.
ISBN 1-930337-71-X (alk. paper)
I. Title.
PS3556.R597A6 2012
811'.54--dc23

CONTENTS

An Inhuman Rival

Third Shot ...1
I was afraid ...2
from Leucopoesia ...3
Mountains Rising in the Distance ...6
Drama, Aug. 4th, 5 a.m. ...8
A Thin Wraith ...9
"and the word is Justice"...10
The Rich Arabian ...11
As the Locust ...12
Small Triumph ...14
Crossing the Desert by Day ...15
August 28, 1973 ...16
In the Inner Sanctum ...17
By Contrast ...18
"marriage of two deaths"...19
Out of This World ...20
The Listener ...22

The Choice

A poem in 5 parts ...23

An Imagined Experience over the Entrance

Oikonde (with 5 parts) ...39
The Great Dream Tree ...43
Regeneration ...45
He (2 parts) ...47
Annunciation ...49

The Window ...50
The Cat Skinners ...51
The Responsible Being ...53
As Bees Breed ...54
Birth ...55
Name ...56
Then Fabled Wilderness ...58
Mid-Wife ...59
As a Drug That Brings Great Relief ...61
The Morning of Death ...62
The World's House ...63
Living in the Open ...64
My Creek ...65
The Landing ...66
The Gates ...68
The Answer ...70
The Wits ...71
Resignation on Rt. 3 ...72
Four States ...74
The Dog Was in the Sky ...76
I Wanted, Then, to Tell You ...78
November ...80
The Rose ...82
Autobiography ...85
He ...86
A One Way Killer (3 parts) ...88
The Archer ...90
First Light ...92
Mother Fear ...94
The Thirteenth Brother ...95
The Refugees (A Dialogue) ...96

- CONTENTS -

I Gathered my Ear from the Green Field

"I gathered my ear from the green field"...99
"I call for someone tough"...100
"The line of advance &"...101
"... as the grass upon the housetops"...102
i.e. ...103
"But listen____"...104
"O God, we need you,"...105
The Rat Knows ...106
"I thot it wd be well"...107
"How we can make it do:"...108
"We saw a bird alight"...110
"Call me as one,"...111
[spider with music] ...112
"Pretense, rage and shame___"...113
"Beyond help"...115
The Silent Call (6 parts) ...116
how ...121
"I tried to say "clown;"...122
Thus ...123
"That thin man"...124
"Words"...125
"(The eyes do not see objectively)"...126
FEVer ...127
"At dawn she compelled us to turn"...128
"We all have someone to whom we express our ..."...129
"We've been pursuing a subject"...130
"Our summer"...132
Kalkaino ...134
Xáox (a bottle of chaos, please.) ...137

The Wildflower ...138
! ...139
The Fancy Little Cur ...140
"*But we stressed living day by day*"...142
"*but it ain't day,*"...143
Beauty is out of Style ...144
" . . . *a lion,*"...145
"*Her thought casts her tendings*"...146
Your Page ...147
"*Peaceful Rabbit with a question mark*"...148
"*Sweet day so cool,*"...150
& I Wrote ...151

A Yelp in the Ideal

Song ...155
The Universe Worm (in 2 parts) ...156
Dawn ...158
A Thin Peel of Moon ...159
Night Fishing ...160
Considering ...163
The Feast ...166
The Island Rabbi ...168
G-d's Law ...171
Revelation ...172
Epic ...173
Standstill ...174
We Were Going to March ...175
Beauty, Beauty ...176
In That Day ...178
Doggerel ...180

Surrender ...183
Black ...184
Life ...185
And for the Homeless ...186
The Valiant ...187
Queen ...188
For Joy ...189
The Song ...190
Voice of Angel ...192
The Tree ...195
The Book ...196
The C Monster In Spring ...197
Truce ...198
But Now ...200
Epitaph ...201
Day Clean ...202
Ah! ...204
Poem In Five Verses ...207

Uncollected Poems

We Leap from a Trap ...211
"Hail, Mary!" ...212
"Our little boat?"...218

for my parents,
my children,
my grandchildren

and for Carl,
The Rabbi of the Islands, himself

AN INHUMAN RIVAL

Third Shot

"I think I'll try another
kind of life," I said mildly,

shouldering my load — light,
I wouldn't carry much.

They brought me a dog then,
a puppy

for companionship, protection —
you know, those things we need. They . . .

"Thank you," I said,
"That was nice."

Shot it twice between the eyes
and left

with only my knife,
no regrets,

no dice,
no toothbrush.

I was afraid

I was afraid—
The invitation read

In peculiar nocturnes:

Hunger
For the Abbot of the Nectarines—

while I wonder,
ponder,
to my soul's service—

compatriot *of all the miracles*

of learning years

from Leucopoesia

1.

It was a claw
But for the sake of the sweetness of voices
we called it wing

It was a claw
which we called wing
stroked into its scabbard

The blade of flesh
joined to the tuberous handle
cut the bindings of language
rubbing in the brain

and freed the drift of long
(long)
silent voices.

2.

The first words she says
after many, many years
are these:

> 'the lens/ is clouded . . .
> my glasses. . . .'

(and the words were *like* glass,
I could see through them
sharp words, sweetened by salt seas)

I said
"Occupation?"
. .
'lightning focused here'

I said,
"Address?"

'number seductive'

Then I knew . . ( ) the Queen.

. .
'The Queen sang zero!' (self-mockery? triumph?)

3.

"introduction to a dream"

Who nodded his head?
The old man blown from glass,
blue, green, white, azure, grey
The beautiful dilution

unfolding and fading
"introduction to a Dream"

At this point/ we begin
                                        coming forward

into the raiment
that they hold for us,

grey silks and watered velvet
like the thaw of snow on dark ground.

Mountains Rising in the Distance

A range of mountains
surfacing on the blade of your sword
passed through me as I died
wounded by too much understanding.

When I remembered that,
clouds lifted,
the final stage of my journey
showed me the palm of its hand:

life-line along the valley trail,
but as the crow flies,
destiny. And I looked out

across a gulf of air
wide as five days' walking:
mountains
rising in the distance.

When I saw that,
a rough plank door swung shut
on the warm light of the sun,
and I am still
until my eyes illuminate the darkness.

I see my wheat stored up
against the wall in linen sacks
as if my one room cabin
were a padded cell of fat years,
and on the shelves, my oracles,
glass jars of pure white flour are gleaming.

In one, to which I give a woman's name,
the humble percolation of the weevil
reads like a book
and I know my enemy.

When will I leave?
How long do I need to get ready?
Sifting flour through my arms and hands,
Midas of potential,
I have time.

Mountains rising in the distance
regulate my breathing.
Sun stored in the unborn bread
enlightens me.

Drama, Aug. 4th, 5 a.m.

the horseless carriage
the one we called The Firefly
comin' down the road in darkness

picks out somethin' with her lights
shinin' like a di'mond

A star......................
the engine trembles .

No one is crowding us,
and the road is so beautiful,
the darkness mild and gentle
the shellfish emerging from the sea . . .

Yes,
It's all comin' back to me now,
the fragile automobile,
the time when we all liked red,
the road winding inland .

A Thin Wraith

A thin wraith
descends the stairs,

That's me.
I'm the blue doll of morning.

I begin to
know myself as

seen in films,
fading and elusive,

I sink back into the grass
like sky.

So I am sky.

But here,
on the stairs at dawn,
I come to give warning.

As the faces of picnickers polished with death
sleep in their reel of glass,
I come to announce my intentions .

You

rise in darkness,
finding your eyes switched in their cradles

and a new persistance stabbing,
stabbing.

❖

"and the word is Justice" –Seferis

What can I pay you with?
The law?

*"The lay of the land is law
The sediment is legal tender."*

Can I pay you then
with dust from the earth,
or the rare striations of insect eyes
that reflect the plain,
the gorge, and the tread of rain
on ice and stone,
the sinking of abundance into a fern,
the fossil of an indecipherable mind?

What can I pay you with? The lore of. . . .
the good life, the lore of home,
the lore of two whom God hath joined?

*"& I can give you death," he said,
breathing death like an excellent price.*

The Rich Arabian

Here comes the rich Arabian
whose wraparounds
reflect your dreams
like oases.

He smiles.
Your spatial awareness
shrivels to a few
grains of salt.

And there you are:
your childhood in a southern town
has followed you
like a dog
too far to take him home,

each incident
a booth in the parochial bazaar
threatening you
with stale cookies.

As the Locust

As the locust split her shell
and hurtled into blossom
        more ardent than the rose,
the lightning
struck the towering pine,
        and bore her heart away.

The shrill-eyed lizard
pulled the cotton from her mouth,
and spoke to the thunder:

"Lord God of the Marshes," (sardonically)
"What a beautiful woman
        you have captured in your net,

lying asleep like an idol carved of green wood
and veined with an inlay of ivory
more yellow than the bill of our youngest egret . . . .

What will you do with her,
lain in your long winding bed
        of the violet and aromatic waters. . . .?

What generation
        will rise from the river
        crying,
            Father!"

Before answering,
the thunder turned his shoulder sidewise
        and rolled his dance of death —

thrice, wrathfully, the net of spindrift
        flew from his fingers,
ffrrr. . . . like fire from a blue magician. . . .

until at last he hauled it in,
his roar receding,
        the casted spell complete

and he himself content to dwindle
shriveled into it like a spider,
        drawing with him the

wind from the trembling marshes

and the woman
        of bone and feather. . . .

Small Triumph

The shoot-out
slithered away:
two men in vests,
a whiff of focus
swelling into the turbulent sky.

I gave wide berth,
scoured my face with slack-jaw,
raised my parasol of the dunce
and sucked the thought of shelter,
the phone booth over there
like an empty soda.

They shot me anyway,
a side issue
like spitting in the gutter.
They shot me for good measure,
hit the coin of my being.

Small triumph:
I keep on walking.
I think that life is easier now.
The sidewalk is like sand.
Light hairs of amazement
test me.

Crossing the Desert by Day

And then the desert
which we had to cross was going to be hotter by day than we had suspected. And we had no shoes, not even sandals, and nothing like a settlement nearby where a cobbler might be found or a last chance souvenir stand with a rack of buckskin loafers.

The streaked, plum colored sands of evening were not, as we could have wished, long shadows from the dunes, but veins of iron which by six the following morning would be unbearably hot.

But we could not face that then and camped in a patch of woods, dead trees with bleached trunks and a few dispirited saplings on the edge of the vast expanse.

Next morning we realized that crossing the desert by day would not be feasible, that we should sleep again and wake in the cool of the evening to travel by night.

June 21, 1975

August 28, 1973

I thought the house was on fire that night. Several times I
opened my eyes to total darkness, or just the faint and less
faint shadow and shadow-of-shadows, the swaying parabola
of the window frame thrown against the wall, transformed
by the curtain swelling and fluttering with ocean breeze.
And when I closed my eyes again and sank toward sleep,
there was the flame, suddenly leaping from the depths of my
vision, my eyes brimming with flame, as if my soul
were burning, and this fire had spread its roots through the
corridors of my whole being, forcing out all consciousness
except the purifying terror of that flame.

In the Inner Sanctum

In the inner sanctum,
the holy of holies,

the acolytes are mules and swine,
squat human bodies
squeezed into these
precious golden vestments.

Behind the massive doors,
in chapels shaped around endurance,

the hoof-held candle
glides like a swan
on mysterious waters.

By Contrast

Snarling and yelping the dog
Strikes for the vein
For miles we can hear it

By contrast cat kills are silent,
Just lulling the arboreal music

❖

"marriage of two deaths" –Annensky

Was it the "marriage of two deaths"
or of the dead and dying?

Surely, for a little while,
life seemed to radiate
and the corpse to inhale
the orange blossoms
and the pall of lilac.

Yes, I saw it—
for a while,
the dying held the hand of the dead,
and the dead delayed
its changing.

Out of This World

Hauled backwards by the scruff of his neck
to a hillside made barren by atomic radiation
and beaten senseless,

he woke painfully,
crept back like a kitten.

Again they dragged him off,
out of their world,
their breath was flammable.
His lashes blazed and died,
soldiers of ash,
like a book of burnt out matches.

A country where only time was the same
lay before him,
and only time had ever been familiar.

He limped to the city.
The street signs, the characters inert,
yielded no meaning.

At first he ate scraps.
Because he had to
there was a sanctity about that garbage.

At last he found work
as a watchmaker's repairman.

A sweetness so irrepressible
it almost shamed him
made him bigger than ever.

The tiny shop was filled with customers,
mostly repairs but some intent on buying.
The townspeople bore fallout with dignity.

He came from the workbench to the front of the store,
unscrewing the jeweler's eye,
the lintless cloth in his breast pocket
like a handkerchief.

The Listener

Disjointedly,
I tell a story
that I hardly understand.

Silently,
you open
your ears.

Without my knowing it,
the keeper leaves the gate,
and all the animals
come forward.

You step back slowly.
You hardly seem to move.
And I forget the time.

Gone blind with innocence,
I stumble after you,
spilling my story
like blond, loquacious gold,
hot coins that burned summer into our eyes forever.

They follow you more evenly,
the animals.
Their hearts are bright apples —
clusters of bright apples —
for they move as apples on one bough,
stirred
by the mild ventriloquy
of silence.

THE CHOICE

In the serious and uttering g(r)asp
of the great spoons of desire,
the first is poetry .

1. The Choice

In the dead of night,
we wake.

The drone of distant motors
tapping its code in the abdomen
detaches us from the sleeping.

From every door we come,
pulling dark robes around us,
eyes marinated in dreams of the home we have left,
to gather on marble stairs worn like a salt-lick
by the feet of transient people.

Now we are free. To go *where?*
Standing where he is, each
makes his own decision; each
silent man and each woman, her nightgown
an unopened morning glory,
stands as awaiting the sacrament,
not waking the old and the children who dream of home,
their faces pressed to the ticking on iron beds.

I *wanted* to go,
but couldn't.

One here, one there,
my children tore me apart.

To go back . . . or to go on . . .
Neither is possible

and nameless men lie upon the floor among the fallen
    bedclothes,
not wanting us to see them weep.

"Sleep!" I cry, "O Sleep!
Sleep of the throngs and masses!"

And raising my eyes to the tall window
where wildly the palm trees blow,

I recall the dream I was awakened from,
the inexorable roar of invasion
breaking upon consciousness like surf

and the voice that cried out in bitter realization,
"Only on the Island can honey still be had,
only in the home we have left behind us. . . ."

Girls with rolled sleeves pack it,
wiping the jar as they hand it across;

and you who have stood there,
transfixed by the motion of a wrist,
the contraclockwise orbit of the scrubbed
and rosy arm round this core of honey,

look up at last,
reach out and accept it,
smiling as your eyes meet hers,

for the *choice* has been made,
the decision was so easy:
the moment of transaction
has taken place.

2. Assimilation

All these sweaters—
holding them, I guess,
though my hands are so long, the fingers
evolved by reaching   into the creature
I am   yet to be

But the children have slipped out of these skins.

This is the second moulting.
Now they go, half-grown and naked.

Following their spoor, we
saw there was blood in it—
blood and nature and those strange ideas

and said to one another,
"He lives the life that you and I lived once and know
from memory." "Yes.
But we lived it in despair."

And I called out,
"When you get to the point that you no longer need us
because you are too strong,
keep in touch!"

But they sailed by,
their lips brushing our cheeks,
their long hair fluttering out behind them
as they took the final steps in the garden, two at a time.

There will be a final moulting.
The human is mated now and
assumes the form of a tree,

revealing its humanness
only after copulation when,
united at the crotch, you draw apart,

sink back exhausted on to the extended limb
which rises from the fork of the tree,

and right before your eyes,
the breasts, the belly, the mons veneris
so fleetingly revealed in the moment of separation,
fade into wood.

Those of us who merge with trees,
united at the groin, as I am to this beech,
or grafted higher up — like Christ among the coconuts,
through the head — cannot move;

but those who are half animal
steal through the night;

Eric has volunteered,
slipping into fox life,

surviving, if at all,
by silence, self-imposed,
his hand across his mouth for a muzzle.

The foxes have accepted him.
He will marry one.

I have been assimilated by the trees,
become one of them,
am no longer recognizably human, can
pass as the limb of a beech

though at first I do not understand this
but lie back, still joined at the crotch, detaching slowly,
feeling myself a bad woman,
while at the end of the street,
clouds boil into the sky .

3. Looking Back

". . . and whatever Adam called every living creature,
that was the name thereof."

"Speech," he said,
"was our undoing, that *choice*,
that breaking of the silence which united us. . .

a refinement of animal noises:
grace notes on the bray, appogiatura of the snarl,
the embellished whimper; pleas and lies and promises
by which we lured ourselves away   from the actual world,

plastering small words upon the scream of the peacock
like leaves to stem a wound.

Even after the invasion,
those who survived — those of us who,
putting out in small boats, made the journey home —

not a moment after we'd crossed the threshold of the
island house,
we were thinking of control:

the six o'clock sentence
and, after.   , the twelve o'clock one.

Looking back on it,
we get a new perspective.

O, I understand the Revolution!
how when we had left for school,
our brown mother (her head bound in rags)
went round to the back of the palace,
not wanting us to see her beg. . .

(and how, when we did see,
we rose up in revolt and fought and fled
and have returned now, survivors of that world,
bringing its corruption with us).

But looking farther back
to the point on the horizon where all lines converge
in that first handful of dust,

how new I was!
dumb and unblinking

'til warm eyes silently told me,
'Why not, Adam?'

the tree rising grandly,
peacocks on the ends of her branches,
the dazzling sun.

And so I spoke,
naming the trees first,
(for I thought I was one of them,
upright and productive,

the words on my tongue the mind's produce,
its natural, spontaneous fruit),

then the birds.
God's hobby in his off hours was to colour the birds
and I named them: titmouse, warbler,
developing signs to describe their activities, abstaining
from unnecessary speech:

 meant feeding;
 meant washing itself;
 meant nesting;
 meant flying away.

O, I sang a little song now and then,
fancied I could lure the moon from His cuticle,

and in the silence that replaced my song
while the sky wheeled round,
spiral it back into His cuticle. . . .

. . . .Of all this dust,
what remains?
Ashes in that silent urn
set as a constellation above a hearth whose fires
are dead."

We were sitting now on packing crates
alongside the dispensary on top of the hill.

"Thus ends catastrophe," he said. Then,
"Do you see? Death is not terrible."

(His eyes, mild and dreadful, put mine to rest.)
"It's only when you compare it with. . . ."

He was looking a little to one side
where ceremonies to the dead accumulate behind the brain.
His head was turned from us and his voice went dead.

"Would you say *response* is what we want?"
somebody urged him.

"Miracle," he said.
And the word awoke us to the moment we were in —
twilight, green, liquescent.

"And if you have never loved love for it," he began,
his voice rising, passion clanging his teeth,

"become utter slaves for it. . . ."
He broke off then.

At his feet a man slept, helpless as a baby
in an ocean of white sheets. Small birds
spattered the air and a woman over there
splashed water in a bowl of flour and began to mix it.

"What *are* we working for?" persisted
one of the personnel. The first

young man said, "Health,"
and touched Dr. Juno's arm with affection.

Press into the body holy the way of all lavish concern

4.

So saying, he stood in the evening air,
in the midst of the evening air,
and cherished the earth.

5. Response

Nothing   got in the way.
No kids with chemistry sets making
snow storms in their father's garage
necessitating us to dig a path to the barn in New

Hampshire. We had time for it, no
excuse, the island providing us with
honey and wild fruit and the influx

of heavenly weather. Nothing to do but
purify ourselves, speaking plainly, say

what we really mean.   For some
it was easy :

the mongoloid, the hebephrenic, those easily given to
divine regression: the pure in heart, the meek, those
surrendering themselves, those plundered
by the throb of mass music.

Now the criminal type also gulps this
sacrament down: the degenerate, the inbred become

as a child drinking milk,
        "Rock'n

    Roll (gulp)

        Hallelujah!"

Genius blown into him (where
the mind has been blasted away),

he becomes a pure vessel,
vacuous and holy, the eyes blown with sky
like air into a wad of molten sand.

For some it was easy,
for others, less. We

worshipped old gods,
proud iron gods:
the motor smuggled in and the whispered dentist. . .

The cardinal, the scarlet tanager (blue-
red and yellow-red): their juxtaposition

(aesthetics! our proud ecstasy) the point at which we
lost ourselves: our art.

We tripped over
roots, left the path, lumbered
through forests, fought progress while secretly
profiting from it, raged

against the ugly buildings over there
with all the violence of which the hypocrite is capable.

I sucked dynamite,
the fuse hooked through my teeth like a cherry stem;

others pull their poor things down upon them
and lie buried in unnecessary rags like autumn leaves

For the peacock's cry is unendurable,
a recantation of its beauty, a gash

in the fleshy air, harrowing as the first betrayal,
the uncurable wound alongside of which all
the offenses against you were lined up,
between us a small table and a telephone by which we sat
on opposite chairs.

"You *do* answer,
don't you?" you said,
though the phone had not rung yet,
the wall-paper stencilled with dream sperm (for we

were wealthy people then) fertilizing
the imagination

as the pendulum

swung back and forth
from yes to no
and back again

And in an unguarded moment, I
recalled

the open cupboard in the upstairs bath
where everything

was a green background
deeper than Thought .

AN IMAGINED EXPERIENCE OVER THE ENTRANCE

Oikonde

1.
Time will erase us_____

Against the wait-a-minute,wait-a-minute ticket,
our brilliance fades.

The mind has three sections.
Two are perpetually present.

But the third is a miner/hammering
the encrusted metal
to claim his liberty.

2.
As moths which weave their patterns into night
(while breath floats outward on sleep's ease),

thought draws a thread, its theme,
which puckers material around it;

unless the *theme*
picked out as a draw string
gathers our thoughts,
what are they?

a life-line's throw-away:
beauty which gasps at the gunwale
and falls back into sweet (and forgotten) dreams.

3.
And the words —
not of one afternoon
but of a lifetime —

they vanish, too —
cards turned up
and tossed to the ground in a careless game

or bottles clipped by the marksman
which shower the empty road among crowcalls.

What *are* words, then,
but wasted breath (a trash of conception)

unless, caught in the colloidal moment,
they hang together as a poem

& fragments of amber glass
suspended in scorching blue air
are crystallized as a vision?

4. Ode to my Greek Dictionary

Nobody noticed
                the edges

where
    subconscious

and the cerebral
began to merge

Like a blue balloon absorbed
in heaven …

                    So,
exploring my nature,

I lay claim to the origins of my language
as to a place,

took what was mine by rights
as oath taking

or as a wife, seized in ceremonial headgear:
the red book, plump and formal
the red book, hot and demure!

5. Oikonde

To show you
the Wonder

I drubbed you, soused, laundered,
baptized you, half-drowned you in

high seas at dusk—
our *language*,

buoyant, profound,
so clear we could see the original meaning:

through surge and backwash
(translations in flux)

it was *homeward, oikade*
(poetic, *oikonde*):
"For Death in his late ships rushed me home_____
the slowly unfolding dark."

The Great Dream Tree

Easter Eve 1980, For Susan

Nuns, unshucked
of their habits, the corn stood in rows.

She slipped in at Vigils,
the prodigal one, reeking
of profane embraces.

Remembering loved ones,
she named them,
assigned empty places:

great spirits, summoned,
crop up like cloud bushes,
sway in an ecstasy of recognition.

"Oi! Oi!" she cries,
the syllable of agony a root,

as in *oikos*, home, *oikonimos*, the management
or disposition of things: the world
she is required to give up
as if death were a season of fasting.

"Oi! Oi!....
It's just that....

with all that abandon
and all that blue,

never to see home again?
the trees? the starry sky?"

The Tree of Light whose seeds *are* stars
springs from this root, *oi*, *oi*,
veiling the field, a dazzling vision.

"I think it could be done:
(dying without regret)."

Regeneration

When the clock was where you
thought you were in a journal,
all the material of the journal, then
was to be allowed to fill up the whole room

(Lines scratched on a glass king's head as,
simultaneous with this,
life seeped into the room in a kind of conception)

•

The attic came to life.

I was looking at an old photograph
which stirred like foliage.

In "I"
the religious mind was crackling.

•

The good,
alchemical child
has steered us with night vision,

and innocence holds me
in starry bondage
like an eyecup of beautiful weather.

But if you ask me
how much gold is in the abstract
crown of a king,

I can only tell you that
the real king was a good man.

Sugarplum visions
run their current of life through us,

and old glass like this,
limpid as artesian water,

was blown from Christmas sand,
and is rare as forgiveness.

He

1.
"The perilous
and still inventive beauty
produce him —

He is through with violence
and a wealth of shelter
breaks from his bones"

2.
The tru, the brutal masochist,
a skirt-like, surgical-blue hood
over the sleek grey snout,

and for eyes
the pink lined slits

like tiny pill bottles of cooked beans
which might go bad if not eaten quickly.

Six months later,
things would go better for him,

and the cable swung
like a heavenly tip in his favor:

the bride's blue satin shortee pajamas
trimmed in deep lace,

her pale Spanish waisted slacks
hung from the sprinkler system.

And with that blue trick
he remembered

the long forgotten rooms
the fine brown dust

in that sealed off apartment
which was his secret.

Annunciation

by Simone Martini (Siena 1284-1344)

I'm armed with savage strength,
savage and competitive as

    red-gowned angel
thrusts and parries God's will,

Mary shrinking into her corner.

"Shall we wait a lil bit?"
Withdrawing into my red hood,
I grin with the snout of the boar,
snagging my tusk on velvet.

I calm myself,
but my organ is really s. . . .,
the sperm to make a Jesus
wildly surging.

Some angels have bugs' heads
like a facial exercise
done in secret.

The Window

The window sill is deep

between the shutters and the soft
transparent
curtain

space

where light is wholly its own
light

a few cubits of air
are lightly resting

Invisible
the child slips into the room
disturbing nothing

his baggage is
arm's length
which travels before him
as if to lay a yardstick on the altar

and this is love

the shaft within the body
lucid
empty

The Cat Skinners

First I ask her,
"Gentle Mother Hulda,*
Kindly let me peel your skin."

I pick at thin grey tissue
until rebuked
"to do it with feeling."

One way to skin a cat
was lifting that thin sheet,
making the bed,
easing the bough of ripe apples.

I turned the bread that cried, "I'm burning!"
and served old Mother Hulda
although she was only a cat,
abandoned and heavy with young
in the cardboard bin where we kept her from escaping.

Some skinners seize the ear or whiskers in strong teeth,
tearing the skin half off in a flash of decision,
and the eyes stare from pink flesh
as a jeweled hand from its glove at the opera;

others slit the belly neatly
and lift the body out
as a child from its bunting .

I was taught differently.
My cat was Mother Hulda
and she had been burned.

To skin the cat
I fit my fingernails beneath dead skin,
"and sensing it could make an unbroken piece,"
lifted the scales from the piano.

* Mother Hulda, of the German fairy tale, for whom our cat was named, is housewife of the underworld. She shakes her featherbeds to give us snow and rewards her industrious servants.

The Responsible Being

...sees pussy willows sheathe curt twigs
as though claws were seed pods....

From that time forth
the kitten warms the earth,

pumps its warmth into cold ground,

dunks its paw in my tea
to thaw the Earth,

dunks its paw in my tea,
a hot compress to resurrect her...

There's soil in my tea
and maybe a little cat shit

dissolving in the cream
from the cow, from the grass,

from the rousing earth,
from the Responsible Being,

and I drink it, trusting
the infusion of paw,

the tincture of sheathed paw
as the tea of this kingdom.

As Bees Breed

As bees breed in the dying king
my father spat them.

Phlegm of wing and shell
clung to my sleeve

when I had carried him upstairs in my arms
light as bread.

"Why do you spit these...?"
And I gestured at the small golden wasp on his pillow.
But he made no answer.

I laid him in my mother's bed,
under eaves.

A cool and sweating cell, as a cistern
deep in the earth condenses moist air,

that room gave me peace.
I shut the door.

Below, my sister in back rooms
expelled a sash of moaning,

the corridors awash,
grey waters swirled at our knees.

Birth

As animals,
(so you) gave birth with ease –
The child spilled into my hands.

I
was a gate to guard you –

The child turned wrong in the womb
came rapidly – feet first.

"Breech!" I screamed,
as though you could halt labor,
return the child.

I feared limbs ripped from their sockets
or the cervix,
knowingly clamped
withholding the head –

But the birth was done,
and the child lolled in my hands,
surging.

Name

To hear my name in water
I leant forward,
fierce
& listening____
It had to be.

My name must run in water,
"Tina, Tina,"
water's small repetitive cascade
from spoon to cup
as though cooling her tea.

"Who hears her name must speak!"
I fought to hear,

pressed past the others,
still as trees in grey mist

and charged my little name
pull its semblance from the miracle.

An ocean spoke____
Upheaval of the sea
drowned
"Tina, Tina,"
Water called my name beneath names_______

My sweet, white bowels hung in the air
like a tree in moonlight,

then life flew from me,
discarding a twisted frame.

Then Fabled Wilderness

The small, thick antlered deer
and primitive swine
come forth from deepest woods
                                        to welcome you,
Our Lady, Our Rightful Lady.
From Tanglewood and inaccessible
                                                black pine
they file in humble as donkeys.

And I, an ancient steward
shuffle through lifeless rooms,
the silt of old bills,
                                    to greet you.

I know you are good and will save us,
return the great domain to its natural order.
Though you come as a childhood rival,
the wild sap rumors peace.
Then fabled wilderness is roused from sleep
And I open the door.

You ride one little deer,
                        still shaggy and matted,
its antlers swollen and dense
                                        as spring trees.

Mid-Wife

All day you scrub the children.
Their knees and shoulders are potatoes dug from clay.

And you are made of sand, dark and wet,
your shape dissolving.

All day at the tub
you are safe and harm nothing,

though sometimes in the tiny stall,
your back to the window,

you crave space and grow peevish,
your teeth like small yellow corn.

And you come to the door
where the view hangs in a colloidal substance

while the rat in loose trousers snores with a whistle,
the faucet is stilled with a wand of light
and the dog is gratified with a potato.

And you contact space
as a dancer braced against glass

while out there a runner stumbles
and catches himself in amazement,

and you rest by the Mid-Power
coming from within and without

as though sinking onto pillows
in a nightcap and white, voluminous gown.

As a Drug That Brings Great Relief

He wore a horse-hair belt,
addicted to the smell of horses,
pressing the plaited hair to his nostrils
like a rope of tobacco,
sucking it in as a drug that brings great relief.

"We know we are dispensable.
We know that if we die, others will take our place.
And it's wonderful knowledge," he said inhaling deeply.

The aroma of horse-hair was almost visible,
trickling from his nostrils and the corners of his lips
like smoke. "Aah," he said,

"You don't have to talk a lot or speak to anyone at all
    unless you want
but may lie like a large naked stone or a gorged tick
dropped from a dog's body in roadside grass."

The Morning of Death

O it had come to the morning
of the drug bitter end

with that quality
of a private bath.

Before breakfast
the sea had evaporated,
leaving mountains of salt

and indecision
    palsied
    the marksman's arm,
endangering everyone.

My mother also,
stepping from the footbath
into her tub. O

these drugs are bitter
and the morning of death,

I feel,
. . . is a wedding.

The World's House

The great house —
every light blazing

as a golden liquor
that will not quench thirst .

The only house in the world
must be in our childhood town

where every street is an island,
a promontory,

and the lighthouse,
in the fashion of great cities,
bugles its emptiness.

No servants in livery
wind coarse cloth around bare globes
to soften the light.

The world's house
burns

in perpetual memory.

Living in the Open

Water falls
down steps
cut into
this
mountain of stone

Plied
with the sad,
inaudible songs
of a different life,
I wash
my clear dish,

reading
the hexagram
of ax
and ripple.

I know this place:
cold pools and boulders,
where leech and crayfish
cruise
through black moss

and the sun
at its zenith
just clearing the peak

drags me
toward its pale
glory.

My Creek

I'm old and laid out like a body, but breath sloshes in me and
I want to take you with me into the slurp and suction, down the
drain, into the sewers of twilight where the pristine Image
skeedadles toward us and steps off into the holy ink of absolute
dark like my father in his baggy swimming trunks, pretending I
was an elegant lady to whom he tipped his hat, so taken with my
charms he forgot to look where he was going and, with his jaunty
hat and yellow gloves and invisible cane, stepped off the dock
and into the dark and voluptuous creek that rose and fell right
under the nose of our house, the creek, hot from the amorous sun
as the purple satin dress on a lady who's been warming her rump
at the fire, a gorgeous princess with emeralds and piled red hair
shocking us all by rubbing her hands all over her haunches and
gurgling with enormous pleasure. That was my creek. Come on.
I want to take you into it with me. Don't ask for a bathing
suit. Just slip out of your clothes, unzip the filmy chiffon
let it slide down your thighs and lie in a heap to receive
instructions from the stinking shrimp net beside it. And you,
by moonlight, its one voluminous mullet, muscling from the net's
throat to catapult back into this element, are borne along on
your side like an odalisque giving yourself to the waters as
trees on the shore must yield to the wind; white birds in
their branches yield too, their topknots fluttering like
candles, single and perishable flames.

Aug. 1979

The Landing

This shade pulled down at twilight
like the Klee painting
    where the sun is a red square,
and darkness falls in a progressively deepening
plaid,

and you feel for a moment
the poetic dimension unfold_____

To eat dust
from picture frames and the lintels of doors,
    obsessed, ceremonial,
a sacrament, yes, death would be a final communion,
flowers before the mirror where you comb your hair
on the landing between two stories with the feeling
    of backstage,
preparing to make an entrance,
or after your exit before you return to the street—
something public
in the confrontation
of self with self-image.

And the flowers are pristine,
the water in which they stand in a glass jar is
    perfectly clear,
the mirror is spotless, the lighting unsubdued.

And the landing between two stories takes on
significance as
a position
as the hyphen
uniting going up to sleep and
coming down to dinner
in a world where
fresh flowers
would come to redress
the knowledge of

irrevocable

decay.

*

The Gates

for Inge

"Lift up your heads, O ye gates." —*Ps. 24*

The gates brought you here,
almost a heart attack!

Through galvanized zinc paint
combustion raged

an ecstasy of rust
attaining sainthood.

Two minutes more
they would have clattered to the ground

becoming human
and all our laws repealed by exhaustion.

But we staved off that time,
exchanging flowers.

Then, what fragmentary story reached our ears?
From what commemorative tête á tête in some other corner
of the room, what act of mercy?

Too easily moved
and bleached of younger women
your face requires nothing.

To turn the tumbler of shyness,
how lost things opened you up:

blue glass on consecrated ground,
the dark alley of telephone numbers,

the perdition
of the unreachable.

The Answer

Sanskrit urchins
curse you,

your golden hair
a nun's hood.

Obsessed
with wonderful discoveries,

the Answer
on the tip of your tongue like a furry bee,

you stalk the dead bazaar
in this habit.

And pollen
dusts the street,

the crumbling arch and yellow walls,
all pollen.

The Wits

Poetic fire-tongs,
the wits:

to seize the molten word
or pluck from the heart's core

some ember of forgiveness.

Of this,
alloyed with irony (for strength!),
the poem is made –

most perfect
when least said.

Resignation on Rt. 3

____Hello, old buffaloes!

The buffaloes are trying to tell me they are *young*____
They groan as I run by,
each remembering the apples
I once rolled beneath the fence.

Their sad, reflecting eyes follow me a while
then turn away.

What else is there to do?
They are not busy.

If it rained,
they could take shelter,
moving with huge lowered heads
to that tin roof projecting from the cliff
which forms one wall of their small pen;

but now they stand
beneath the August sun,
their coats like rotted carpeting,
snuffling dry earth,

mother, father, sister
(or, perhaps she is an aunt or second wife)
and this new one
(a mini-taur!)

who skips
with the expectancy of youth___
life stretching out before him!
executes an awkward experimental frolic,
inviting his unresponsive aunt to play.

Then,
as from his father's bulk and sigh
there wafts the sense of some great teaching

he moves close to his mother
and grows still.

Four States

(on the correlation of sight and music)
For M. S.

I'm playing my piano in the Balsams,
on a high and open crest,
gazing out across a sea of hills and plains.

My hands span octaves.
as I contemplate the view –
as music and as vision stir each other fundamentally,

and the great, sheer chords
which spread the valleys out
and have displayed the hills

rise through my bones,
rise up like sap from the hard stone bench
on which I am sitting

and fall lightly
from my stretched, inspired fingers
to stagger from the upright
like evaporation,
like shafts of mist in sun...

And the old man with me
who has hobbled on blunt feet,
bearing this instrument,

attends the spare, momentous and occasional
great music which induces vision

and then points out,
"From here you can see four states:"

and he turns, his stiff arm reaching,
"Georgia, the Carolinas, Tennessee."

The Dog Was in the Sky

The Dog was in the sky, and I,
guiding my small craft by literature,

felt Deneb in The Swan glide by
and then, dark feathers fanned my face
as silently we raced The Eagle.

Such perfect stillness
isn't anyhow for man or beast.
The animals have gone into the barn.

But for myth,
silence is best.

Raking now from Milky Way the autumn leaves,
I saw imprinted in the sky
the stars of Hercules' long thigh
running across the heavens,
striding toward the west forever

and I thought,
"As a sedative, their balance,

as pieces of a larger picture,
the balanced stars."

They say to be forgiving
and to forgive all.

if that is difficult
(and that is all),

there is *won*derful solution
in some of the stars,
lonely and proud.

As writers screen rivals,
my sincere thanks to the heavens!

Even in the clouded night,
the stars pressed through

to print peace upon me.

I Wanted, Then, to Tell You

I wanted then, to tell you
how just before it ended

it was perfect, perfect –

the way a dying person
can transcend old grudges –
agonies and hatreds
like swollen and exhausted leeches
falling away.

Everywhere,
from branches
and the pure lines of chrome tubes
young men chinned themselves,
smooth, respectful,
trimming off the last superfluous ounce____

and a cry rang out –
a child called to her brother
across the snowy field
and the whole sky trembled slightly.

It was twilight,
cold and glowing,
just the color of *morpho* wings,

and the note resounded

as flesh became "The Word,"
the soft, pure gold of an illuminated text
as it was in the beginning
before heaven and earth
had been formed.

Dec. 1980

November

... the grey chitchat of early morning,
low barometric interludes
sucking the windows,
and dawn swung open..

..
We woke in our sober nests
that grey November morning
and whimpered for summer,

but the tree held up its barren limbs
and swayed against the Sky
in a gesture of impotence.

We had seen the harvest,
and the blessing poured down like sun
on our haystack of beautiful artistry,

but now, the last of our own sweet corn
lay in the dingy grocer's,
stripped to its final husk
and marked down for rapid sale:

and it hurt to see it as those
perishable years of our lives,
the melons no longer in season.

Yet we woke in the dark bush of winter
to find one twig was leafing . . .

and while "ambivalence laughs
at this sprout of the holy grail,"
the unexpected species
that bursts into leaf out of season,

as Sarah laughed, saying,
"God hath made me to laugh
that all who hear will laugh with me,"
perplexed at bearing Isaac in old age,

we took it as a sign of hope,
accepting hibernation.

The Rose

The rose in our river is dying
All it can do is cry, "Who will help me?"

& I said,
"What we need is a short barrel."
But he said, "No,
it will do no good.

If night comes
& darkness

running as a man
in a sarong/ which binds his legs

running slowly,
a white sarong
drawn through the legs
as in the Byzantine pictures of Jesus,
constrained
in these parentheses of clothing,
what then?

I pressed my thumb between your eyes,
but you still felt so much hatred,
a girl I mistook for a garden .

        But let us achieve -
        because (not yet achieved) the spiritual (   )
        will be a great bonfire
as early (or at death)
as the reverent task stealing through newspaper (like flame)

You kissed me once on the lips

You called on me many times
You gave in abundance centavos and dimes
which were misunderstood

Your uncle knew and loved the rocks of this country
as though it were a pet's backbone."

And he said to me,
"If people are still smoldering,
why aren't there any other creatures
                    to feed healthily upon,
                gain grace and knowledge?

On this side of the mountain, we wash the gods_____"

I have a happy ending_____

As divers who sway in the backwash
proceed from the depths
                            bearing beautiful money
                    like The Cup in its hut of black velvet
I carried the rose
                who spoke knowingly:

"Now there are some born out of peace
& their exuberant tradition will not be forgotten
(*exuberant* as ex uder, from the udder, the full breast)
Examples are
                                        the scalding blush of a virgin
      & the grub's calligraphy in bark.

Others have no birth
They spring from a sheet of rippling tin
as flowers shatter the air when the still mind
is startled by thunder

& night is a picture book
where the Virgin's chin is a sow's belly
and Christ holds the world like a red apple_____"

Autobiography

My first pet was a spider!
My toys? Shadows!

An infant,
I lay on the floor — no rug!

Light nourished me.
I loved clean boards.

My mother prepared me a basket,
anxiety lacing her bodice —

This mobile of shadows and web
hung over me, transfixed
as a dog to its bone,
as an old man riveted to his jabbing.

And I prophesied the time when I would be old,
chained to an ivory bed,

obsessed with the net woven from her body
as a man for his freedom.

O, it took time to come to so much richness
though the jewels change and I shift color
as dragonflies hatched in twilight.

It takes more time,
unfolding like a rosy quilt, to dispose of it.

He

When he saw
that the past was his shadow

he passed into the path
where they cut down feet and hands that are kicking and
   grasping
as logs trimmed for the river,

where time seems less substantial,
& winter floats out like a curtain filled with spring.

Already the woolens fade____
things do not freeze so____
year-round cotton flutters at our ankles
& an old woman's face at the window
reflects confusion.

He had one great passion.
But that passion was to escape this shadow!

And he swept with a will
as though dust were shorn fleece
and the ordering of one's affairs were liberation.

When he saw his life was complete,
he cried out,

"It is no bigger than a coin
trimmed with darkness and a thread___"

& I weep for joy____
such a sentient creature____

as the great tree,
turning gold at the end of summer
offers itself___

The leaves ripple
                    in an unexpected wind

And the old man
totters back to his house
shaped like a walnut, uttering,
"But we are human,
but we are human!"

They've made him a party
but he's escaped into the night
where the skies are sprinkled with seed
and the fields are weedy as his beard___

and the royal..
and The Royal..
and The Royal Guests
enter the gate, lifting the loop of bent wire,
their shoulders brushing the rose .

A One Way Killer

But look, Little Boy, you hero,
I have almost found you, hiding

1.
A one way killer,
death in the idyllic
that it takes you a moment to find,
a close-up of the dazzling canvas
and two lines of black dust
that merge to form a human.

Then you must tell them
    of fairy dust
    that neutralizes this,
the road map of crumpled foil
and the golden message of age,

the spatulate gold fingers
that hinge the black volume.

2.
Lilah Fisher came from the South,
a black, "most-wanted" woman.
She used this pseudonym
to fight for freedom.

But Vera meant Truth.
It was *this* name,
torn from her by the roots,
that hurt her now.

Her daughters rose from their pillows at midnight,
their long, unbraided hair spread round their shoulders,
and listened with apprehension.

The wide oak-paneled door,
stalwart and mulatto,
in the downstairs hall where a light was kept burning,
spoke to them in their mother's absence,
the sour, wry talk of an old nurse
mustered in their defense.

3.
In the quiet evening
how the boogie man rose up like vapor,

the lozenge-eyed half-god
dissolving in the air by the corner grocery
where a man had once been murdered.

Just under the surface of night
the city hangs like a trap or a sodden timber;

the sense of not knowing
runs in your belly like hunger:
but you have come for this:

The ante-bellum houses are baited
with an irresistible childhood.

c. 1970

The Archer

> "It was said that he who was very strong
> could bend the bow,
> but we did not think anyone could bend it."

Now the young man
who had stirred to the echo. . .

was aghast to come across
the poor pale corpse in his forest;

a child lay face down on the ground
in a blue work shirt and black suspenders,

and, though there were no marks of fang or claw,
he thought he had perceived
a white bear leaving the body.

A huge tree lay felled
at the entrance to the woods

where children whirl,
the pink, inhuman shadow
dancing among them.

And, as a child who slips the bonds of brotherhood
to try in quiet rooms
the pure sombrero of death,

the great sheer locust
soaring upward
scatters small flies.

First Light

Rising from the broken knife,
rising from the sheath of night,

rising from the broken air,
rising from the Pity Heart of man,

light!
light poured salt on a bird's tail,

touched my face in the stylized grimace of labor
as though memory caught light,
a snapshot undeveloped for eighteen years.

The channel seen in first light
was a silver scar

and daylight advanced, accepting
the pink, salt-stiffened towel
on a rope beside our mirror.

Red-winged blackbirds gleamed like a flung holly wreath
and blackbirds patronized the senile fence
limping out into water.

Rising from grass gone to seed,
the path overgrown along marsh,
some grey birds were feeding.

To capture everything, my shadow moved
stealthily before me like a butterfly net.

In this path of never trimmed leaves
moisture found its keep:

even in drought, the earth beneath scrub myrtle
was cool and silent.

Mother Fear

"The beautiful doomed rose-leaf notebook!"
With a cry she sprang from her chair
and fled the room.

Yes, beautiful___
the phantom mandala,
the binding of carved wood,
light, aromatic wood . .

The watering can was a face in distress.

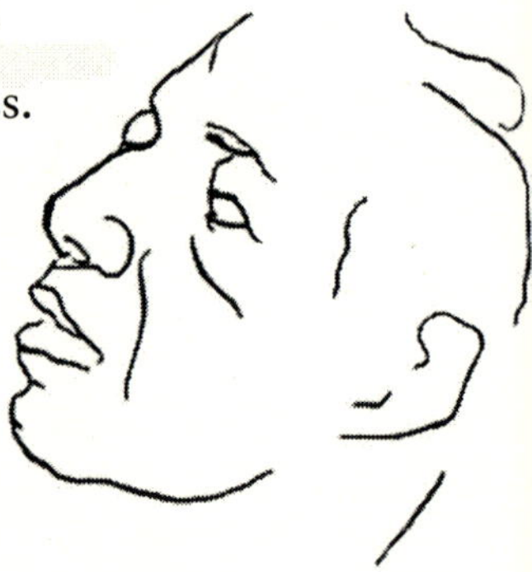

Now gentle, earth-stained fingers
dust the rose,
the growing data of pregnancy,
a folio of landscape seen
as children dare to be truthful. .

"The beautiful doomed rose-leaf notebook!"
She sprang from her sunken chair of blue-grey lawn,
intra-uterine rage spilt through the articulate mouth.

Deterioration
was her first earth,
her first terror.

The Thirteenth Brother

..: to find in night's convertible garments
a vestige of slumber:

the thirteenth brother's
feathery embrace
as, nettle-sweatered,
drags the enchantment with him;

thunder of massive wings
and I rose to welcome them,

hurling the stinging shirts as they came,
one by one and stood before me,
men, tall and strong,
stained with the blood of my fingers.

"Was there a bullet?"
"No, my brothers, there was none."

Six years I had not spoken,
the words clad in silence
rocked in the glowing tissue of regeneration.

But they stood
pale as from deep anesthesia, and
knew no more the lofty element.

The Refugees
(A Dialogue)

The Daughter: (dreamily)
You were looking at me
through some kind of cathedral

where the wind ran wild
through flourishing grass . . .

The Mother: (sharply)
This soil is poor as sarcasm,
our garden a landscape of carrots and shards.

Your boyfriend is rootless and anemic
unintensified by culture
a field of blue flowers
        sprouting from the web-covered dung,

unintensified by the echoing helmet of teak,
the double vision of the masters.

Unlike us,
he has not sprung from the earth of amazing
        countries,

and though it is evident in our teeth and our
        nails,
our brains and our suffering
that we will end up like most of them,
with bloody noses, with grey faces,

the scarves at our throats in rags,
still, you will find us
scrubbing our knees like clay-covered potatoes—

While the pale men
sleep
folded unconsciously upon the earth,
we lie on our backs
our eyes glued to the perpetual eyes
        that illumine our darkness.

I GATHERED MY EAR FROM THE GREEN FIELD

❖

"That twilight which has made anchorites of kings"
—Helen Waddell in her preface to *The Desert Fathers*

I gathered my ear from the green field

&, lively, encounteréd
those rooms   when they were

j u s t   t w i l i g h t

He was investigating now
into its origins,

believing that the Light came___
And that maybe things
had opened up___ that compassion
may have opened up

the world immersed in cold
like a lesser jewel

❖

I call for someone tough
when I take the expansion moth

and raise it
and gather it into an assembly .

Do we really want
to give ourselves
(this crumb of life)?

I need to ask you,
Where did such a lovely sweater come from?

It comes from the heart.
We have to pull the wool in long strips
from the heart

and knit away
this life .

❖

The line of advance &
the line of retreat
supplied for them
an evolutionary system
hard to fathom

and take me
to the edge
of outer space
where I'm not
supposed to go

which covers
in one peculiar outline
the end of all worlds
and the beginning

From there
one could be lost,
be lost utterly,
be utterly lost

—this incredible
jigger of dark
i'm not
supposed
to finish—

& only now do I realize what luck I had . . .
& only now do I say *t h a n k y o u* .

"... as the grass upon the housetops ..." ps. 129

ps. 129 —
a brown sea
the basic elements
do not change,
and the stars have not
collapsed above us —

What is
sees itself,
gives up —

"There'll be many along here
dead before long"

The elements retain their
quality of wet, hot, solid —

The air is .

i.e.

Virginia, i.e.
it is adorable that it shd be translated that way
on uncut pgs.,
a
fat/little book   and, Ah!
that you shd want me (i.e., the Southern "*I*")

to open it
& thumb the blank
vellum .

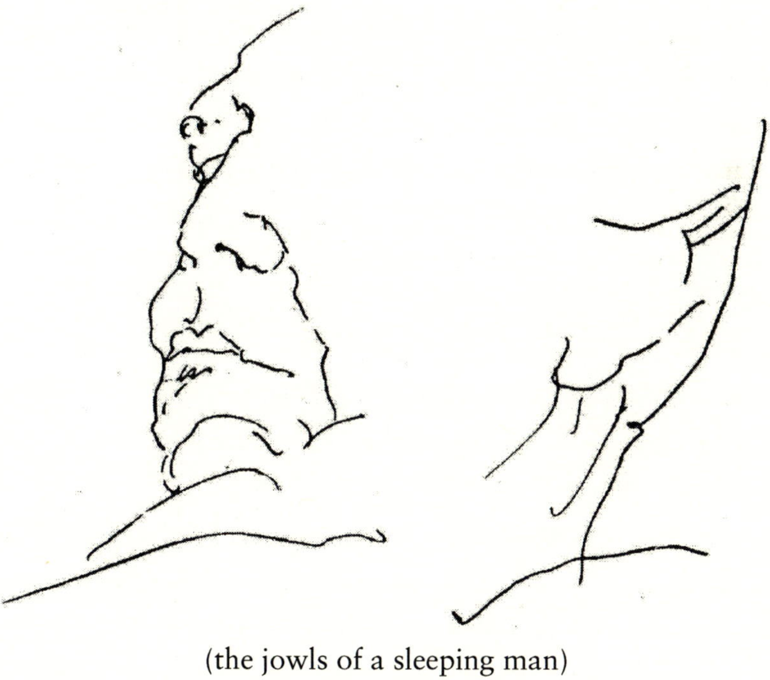

(the jowls of a sleeping man)

❖

But listen________

If we can't enjoy ourselves,
we'll take our flashlight
to the target

And the hideous girl,
when she learns of God's love,
will use a special beauty

because she's not stupid.
And our tiny light
nuzzles the dark

to pore over some animal___
a dog's furry snout
or the cat a little way off

And I travel there___
into the east Mother
and to the West

Hello, Sweetheart!

❖

O God, we need you,
trapped in your emptiness,
a different type of nothing
which,
if we mention it,
(proves only)

that there can be a dippy productivity
which results from so much
stripping away of understanding.

So, hallowed be thy name-root.

❖

The rat knows
without question
the house soup
must be tasted
even   if only
for the sake
of human value

and I
am just so happy
to learn
my lesson
in this life .

and you who tasted
and said it was too salty,

and you who looked
but did not see the light,
let the white banner flap!

Let God, if he exists,
prepare for us our huge glory

where the drowned kittens are safe
his black hands smothered with rings.

❖

I thot it wd be well
to set up God with his penis
& ignore the dark-

ness .

Mister God also sets up
without asking the rights
of any person .

I
(wd have) felt foolish if,
at   end of   day,
had searched for her
ruby in the dust

so
(I)
put out my hand,
poor Love,

to the falling rain .

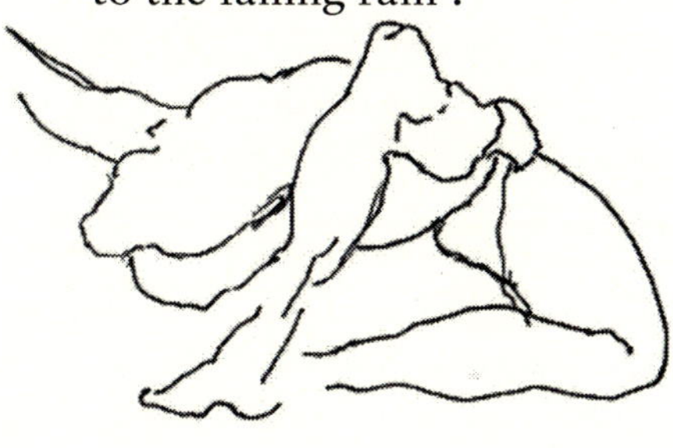

❖

How we can make it *do*:

We could
eliminate
the high quality (bis)

ride into
dark spaces

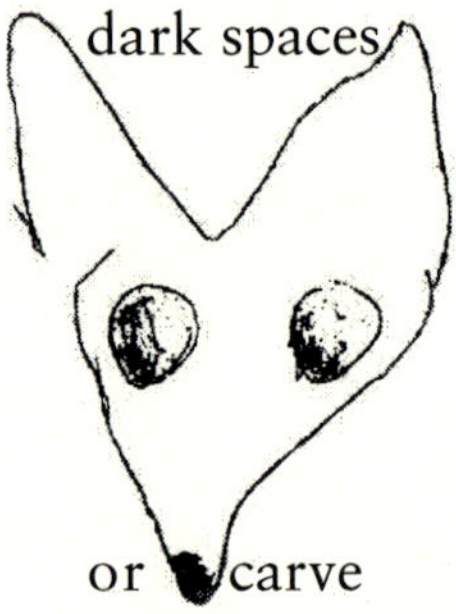

or carve
an idol in black stone

to build a bigger (concept
of the Universe) accentuating form .

Why don't you and the kittens come home with me?

•

See? she knows this (The polish hygienist)
and the quiescent mood
    just around the corner

And what is this
elemental goo
que vous avez appuyé sur ma maison
whereby we get a little extra___

See? If I had to change my mind,
I'd find (in the changing)

an extra
today .

❖

We saw a bird alight
in the primary colors of childhood .

So praise may not be enough
to penetrate this wonderful nook just now .

Praise is weak
and flattery is nothing .

Talk without them,
walk about the soul for

Nothing

"The red,

red bird," the mother said, fingering her baby's ears,
"its long wings dipped in blue".

❖

"Call me as one," she
says, "whose body hangs
suspended
from the burn mystical,

unburned
but tried
by the extending heat .

Eggs of the fly,

caught in *amber*
the *Beautiful*

hang with me,
brocaded into Being,

(cool to the cheek) .

Call me as one whose secret voice
is tuned to the ill

who lie swooning before her spacious emptiness

whose
clean white labor
(was) to lay her head
upon the ground .

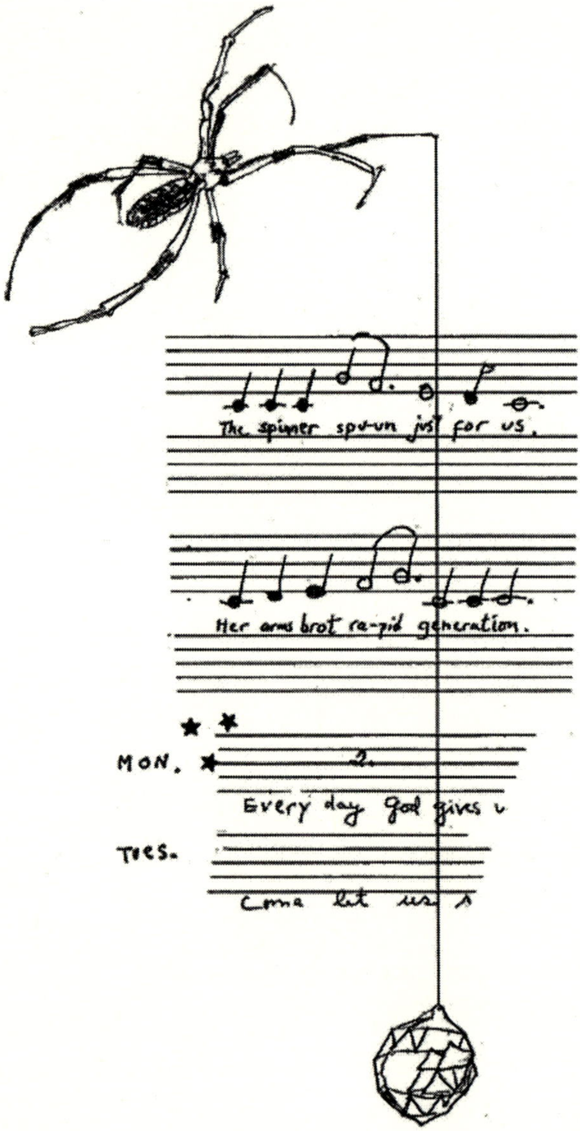
The spiner spu-un just for us.
Her arms brot ra-pid generation.
MON.
2.
Every day God gives
TUES.
Come let us

❖

Pretense, rage and shame___
I had brought them under me
as a horse of wind .

Death would no longer give himself
to a throng of idlers,
letting them fill with hatred,

but come only at night,
in a piney grove,
making them fill with shame .

He shows, invincible, points of the truth .
And all the different points are nakedness___

The naked truth .

.
In the shadow,
in the shadow cast from promises,

we tried to drink deep,
crying, "Air! Air!"

And the sun cast its tall bronze
where an inconspicuous small shrub

is sweetest and most victim .
And the shrub cast its small island of absolute dark

and I, myself, was frightened__
as if I had seen something, a

foreboding behind the shadows of the flame,
an angel, yeh, you are surprised?
I was frightened and ashamed .

And the Angel set before me a book of colors, dazzling,
whose pages I turned backward, perversely,

receiving their light upon the lids of my closed eyes
with a shudder of ecstacy

And he asked me,

Can you see?

And I said, "Yes." But he rebuked,

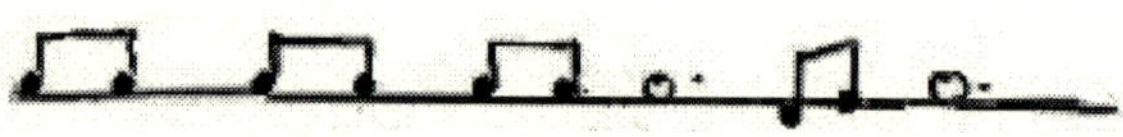

"Why don't you look at the whole human being?"

And I found in looking a word *bold* on my moral edge,

"Come forth in matters of thought."

❖

Beyond help
from my fellow man,

I have ceased all activities__
Activités.

When the horse stopped, I thot,
it will hurl me in every direction.

But you need, you know,
such *faith* .

The early part of the night
becomes clearer at the end .

And we welcome . . . we welcome?
we *welcome*
Night

and trust you may find
a clear

image .

The Silent Call

I.

She always wanted to be
clean, amenable.

She was familiar
with that great look of beauty
that enters the Silent Call,

stood looking out through the dark screen
to where three fledgling goshawks
perched in the crotch of a swarthy tree.

One adept with mercy
would not have let them range in the deep yard,
spanish moss, their muscular thighs,

but in a wire hutch have penned them in.
But she stood still,
imbued with the Great Look,
not touching the dark screen,

knowing when it opens,
she'll be locked in again.

(*I* believe it.)

2. The Seer

but, O! the lightning in the language
to which thought rises!

The xerox
    I once considered
"born with a caul"

slips under his lid,

the light of his intelligence flashing.

He could copy the Ideal
and if he did,
the stones and grass
would lie in sequence.

But some are lost to the computer
who might have been claimed by the Dream,
a thin, superfluous mathematics,

and the same day they
made him a
football hero, yeah!

and when they are all together,
and when they are all together,
(   )ing and cheering....

It's just too hideous
It's the nuts of forbearance,
darling,
to try and fail and try and never get him

O dear, o dear, o dear
How deeply I
loved, I

3. Deus Absconditus

those tubes of devil-colored light
which make pain immersion

kept rubbing my eyes,
blinded by illusion,
so different from
the spilled *panier* of flowers

we could not but conclude
God made himself to be

driving off with your mother,
a man of beautiful blue eyes

You can call him if you like
but you must remember this is
an after school center
not some seventeenth rate king of kings,
hysterical and the holy unguent

O roi de mon coeur!
Comment l'eau forte a coulé vers moi
de ta couronne?

4.

Has she always been so fat?

Not really. Her thighs have been pushed
from oysters into hams
,devouring a whole pack
of softened hearts.
while reading the tea leaves.

We spoke of the Great Enigma then.
There is no enigma, she said
but a broth of trees

And would, in fact, you say/that Satan owned the world
by classifying it as a red mobile?

No. But I have run to see you, unbearable,
enabling me to crack the code of the world in space
(which has) the Father in disheveled clothes
lurking with the broken spirited

5.

He lurched out of the darkness toward me
his face concealed by
a prepuce of loose rags and she
(by now she could not but be conscious
that he was thinking of her)
blundered into a cul-de-sac,
followed by a dozen men

And now it seems to be the kind of fantasy
we all want to hear: ectoplasm...

6.

Amino, transcendent amino,
which opens into

night and day
sloth

how

The *page!*
The *page!*
that it bend
that it *bend!*

that it adhere
to light beyond it,

a cosmic thickening
of brilliance

as you can see
in a sensitive and delicate
stove.

When he began to take control,
he noticed more
and more

    how
everything
was thought
    and (seen)

through such means
as b*rrr*illiance .

❖

I tried to say "clown;"
but the word came out "trout."

"I'm also a trout," I said.

Male Voice (slow, dull):	In which *things* . . . , uh, puppy-dogs, are . . .
Female Voice (brisk, crisp):	. . . guarded like a silver fish

Thus,

Without the poem
I could not comprehend
the language .

Nor could I
celebrate its Plato
and ceremony .

Thus,
the symbiosis of bison,
insects, bats—especially in summer .

But with the herd's destruction,
they will no longer
be transforming

essence
          in the presence
of insect juvenilia

essence in
the presence
of
insect
juvenilia . . .

❖

That thin man
in his room
on the top floor
which he calls home,
what does he do?

He lives there,
intensely,
with the idea of the wireless
not having one.

There's not much in his room.
He keeps it swept and clean.
He lives the way he wants.
A blue figure in the snow.

Says hello to the people around him.
So he makes his country
our country.

❖

Words
like a cloud of gnats
surround me,
an allegorical figure,
holding,
as my sign,
a rusted window screen
through which sky seeps.

Now this interests me
because it speaks of spaces,
filling up

and it's awful
because it has no intention .
And an armful of
laundry has nowhere to go

and the genuis of young women
long, long gone
haunts me still

and a toothbrush
stands in a glass of water,
its stem refracted,
here,
on the sink.

❖

(The eyes do not see objectively)
but the beauty blooms from them

As we have seen,
God threads himself through seven eyes
in the course of a dream.

However, I am going to say, "As clouds
sewn over the face of the moon,
(is beauty concealed)."

FEVer

I kept looking in the mirror .

This was the homeopathetic gaze,
it was The Foundation of the Ending
of the World of Vanity,

the base, (*hypo-thesis*,
or under-standing) from which spring
(*thesis* and *anti-thesis*) the real
self and the contradictory, false "I"
converging in the (medicine) chest,
iodine-tinged eyes,
peroxide boiling in the wound like a soul) .

And yet,
the imagination continues to assault me__

Pretty good for the imagination!
He sneezed me right out of the room!

❖

At dawn she compelled us to turn
and walk into the lovely mirror,

to safeguard it, all things being told,
a *little* blaze to warm himself!

But the more he spoke, the more phrases he learned
until his mastery of selfhood was complete,

and he could penetrate dawn
which we define
as "anything happening"

if we can get around
the Laws of the Positive,
the gospel from which she was struggling
now to escape .

somewhere we can go
we *can* get there together!

and took a divine
nap .

❖

We all have someone to whom we express our concems:
I am God's face-clock.

Wound by an angel,
how shall I *not* time tell?

And if, without asking,
a white moon occurs

and the whole poem appears,
neither embarrassing nor funky,
with the sense of a little victory,
the sense of my real concern,

then I am progressing,
moving in slow time with musical interludes,

with that lurch of the shy bride,
that backwash of the incoming sea–

"(   ) the patience, the sacrifice, the integrity_____"
What does it mean?

My life ends in one mood or another.

I shall drink   memory .

❖

We've been pursuing a subject
I'd like to continue this evening:

how the Soul is hydrolysized, A and B:

A. You can have a *bé-bé*
who is greeted in the morning room
as bearer of the light.

B. As the old woman, like the dog,
wants still more attention,
scratching behind the ears and so on

(for they don't serve a micro-usable person here
and there's probably someone giving them big tips
and making it tough on the rest of us

and it is hard for her to get to sleep
or to have a little dream
and there's no creative prep-talk
to make Death human,
shabbily dressed but so pretty
as you or I am),

you can breathe in the same breath.

See? *This* is what I feel :

I hear the Earth's irradiations
modifying who we are,

snowflakes moving south from Buffalo,
one with a tiny bit of scruff under its fingernails.

Goodbye, Children!

❖

Our summer

reclassified
as ◡ nice ◡ dark ◡ turf

on which float

many elements

Mix with the elements
OOF! our sister-in-law
So it's back to the

oof!
There is no hope of
generosity or compassion
just a little bucket on 4 wheels
so that
if a person wanted more,
he could start cleaning his body
& should enquire,
continually enquire . . .

And yet . . . ?
life has moments . . .

Now   to backtrack
        in a modern
         mixture

in no particular poetics where the world moves,
        1000 flies moving

this & this & this

Καλχαίνω

> **kalkaino**, I seek for the purple fish; *metaph*. I search in the depths of my mind; I ponder deeply. *The Classic Greek Dictionary*, prepared by George Ricker Berry.

(A man and woman cross the street
with a book in her hand.) It said,
"You can look in the garden
and in the land."

It said,
"She stood still,
open to the wind."
(The wind plays on the surface of her mind.)
Let's make this a test case.

She stands on the corner,
an empty volume in her hand,
an empty reality in her mind,

and as she thinks of letters
and of writing them, words,
like a school of fish,
darken the corner of her mind
(dart across the corner of her mind.)

"I'd be afraid to show them to anyone, surely,
but it doesn't mean I shouldn't write them down.
'In the garden,'" she writes, "'so beautiful
(with its sickening domesticity),

you choose a daffodil, you don't need the rest
and lay it on the surface of your mind.'
I write in the abstract answer about things."

Now we're going to talk about the Louisiana
Purchase, the Geneva perch and the Treaty of
. . . : Cover the oven-proof dish

These are the basic states
and they go through (
) to this Ideal.
We have just had a perfect afternoon of questions.

•

"O, Summer Dove, I've gone downhill." (He shows his gums).
"He shouldn't have let you get in that condition," she says,
"When's the last time you went?"

This is husband and wife. (He looks in the window
where books are displayed like dead butterflies to please him.)

The wind blows on the surface of her mind.

"I think it is so sad! things are so sad!
It's just that things . . .
God! Children,
life is our one chance to respond to anything,
the polka dot skirt with halter top, but if
,for some reason, you don't want to do this,
nine pigs
will be removed. (This is the withdrawal of the senses).

Come! Let me go alone, just I,
while the dead of night is spread out against the sky
like 9 piglets euthanized upon a lab tray."
(She floats upon the surface of her mind).

:__I don't know how you . . . No, no. This is not . . . No.
Anyway, swimming out there is not nice, the water is polluted
& (you have a dirty mind).

:__The words of (   ) in Persian I render, true.
But the fact is it's nice, untouched,
and the thoughts are just as fresh as shrimp!

:__and it's yours, but it's never going to get us home,
it's like suicide . . , like . . .

:__ Lord! it's sexy!
(She snorkles in her mind.)

And so a pleasant (   ) from Feed the People
and don't show me any second-hand information.

Χάος

She (housewifely): A bottle of chaos, please.

He (in vicious imitation): A bottle o' chaos.

She (protesting her innocence): . . . the natural-born final act of mothers______! So our bodies are hung with wide open sketch

The Wildflower

"Full many a flower is born to blush unseen,
And waste its sweetness on the desert air." —Thomas Gray

There is a shy wildflower.
It is found in the woods
in early spring

with (luck)
and a total inhibition against

trampling
the pregnant ground.

This inhibition
leads to a spring
and the power to go on,
the power to find others.

The lily hides,
participates.

Of course the scheming lily
begins life in crystalline involvement,

but I have never seen one that didn't lead you on,
to waste its essence on some tourist
for silence is the essence of therapy .

Its essence is always being wasted.

!

It invites direct experience, the sun
leading us on

It invites
the two-tailed pony

(her golden, clockwise orbit!) leaping
the fence

delightful! delightful!

delightful! delightful!
delightful! delightful!de lightful!
delightful! delight ful! delightful! delightful!

The Fancy Little Cur

"Thirst," I said, "thirst. I thirst."
An economy of words was my reason.
"I thirst," I said. / How to explain?

The misery
the cold misery

in this northern part of the world where
snow-whitened hills are spangled with red
berries and groves of sumac with fruits of
dried blood

and the roads
laid out in square miles
enclose our lots
where stone and rubble
crop
through snow .

Here, at the corner lot,
where the asphalt road is poured

like the cover of a bible,

a roll of plastic webbing to zone
off a dump site leans

against the fence
and holds it
up .

And the house,
should we ask its value,

is worthless .

But the fancy little cur who dances at the end of her chain
is the reason I got turned around

For here,
at the cross roads,
where the orange guard stands propped
and the little dog barks at the end of her chain,

I thirst

And the dust is huge
& the unmetered ultrasonic

of sound .

But we stressed living day by day
until one day

but it ain't day,

just the day of my tongue
with its written, uncanny

architecture

Beauty is out of Style

But Beauty is Beauty
not merely
for the sake of the imagination _________

It will be beautiful in part
          to act some merit
          to act some deed of signal darkness
according to its use.

But Beauty is out of style now,
through pistil and into ovule
where the seed is set.

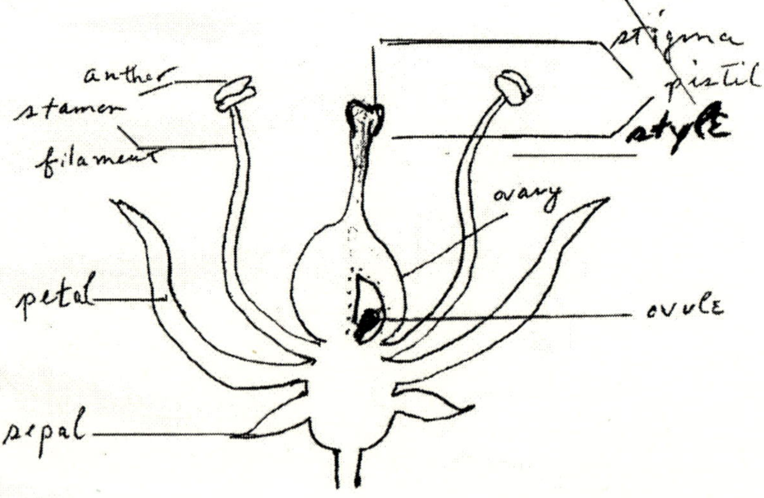

an octopus disguised as
diagram of a complete flower

❖

. . . a lion,

slowly, slowly,
the door swings open .

He finds himself in absolute bliss, in
absolute wonder .
H u g e , f r a g r a n t d a h l i a s

those who believed so firmly God should have a cause and a cause and effect and affect events and reflection . . .

Early, early, you got visions
. . . that everyone didn't see

insight into two children reading the gospel in
Icelandic: duwer wist Heem

•

What have you seen recently?
Details into the glory of the dream?

•

Have you looked for methods to put in ,supplement ,depress ,forgotten it ,substituted movies

,the silence ,the lack of communication

•

If I annoy you I will leave at once

❖

(Voice) :Her thought casts her tendings
on this, her levers__
and the balance tips .

Pure thot. . .

(Para-voice) :*Pure thot?!*
(Voice) :Yes, pure thot___(not tough ugly thought, but)
such a limpidity as
children sometimes share__

sings
with a skewed voice

(Para-voice) :O, *linguige!*
so, now you gotta change the oil
& check the hydrolic fluid,

the tiny little light bulb,
shinin' like the Red Sea
like roses among garments

fláme, fláme__
annoint his body
i n   e t e r n a l   f l a m e

Your Page

"That is the last of . . . ," you said,
"That is the . . ."

The North fell away a little
where you were looking,
your lips slack .

so we went, 1000 strong,
to see your work in a city without rails,
not even a hotel,

only the hospital,
its vaulted walls of esophagus-red brick
where you lay with your deadly infection,

the blistered lips I longed to kiss,
hovered like a hummingbird above hibiscus,

a brimming beaker of pure water beside the bed .

And at the end,
I didn't know (the rest)
but standing beside the grave in plain sight
is a huge daylight binder

and your page (its proofs)
is profoundly

your page .

But what'll I do with 'em now?
O gosh .

❖

Peaceful Rabbit with a question mark .

.

Sometimes it's worse than others____
How and Where

All we can do is

At least you tried it!!
We've all become so---

---*much*

The calmness of the hands,
the elementary   silence .

All we can do is
offer our misfortunes to the Golden Light
til we have reached a heroic Consciousness
of Order and Mortal Pain

and of
How Limited the Sea is
"this the

day I do not know?"
are words with which we bid farewell___
Peaceful Rabbit with a question mark
Our very paradoxical

departing .

"Sweet day so cool, so calm, so bright,
The bridal of the earth and sky;" —George Herbert

Dump the (laundry) on the lawn
And keep the Keeper in my swoon

Whatever I convert to lyric thought
Belongs within the onion

And if I could
I'd try to find

Herbert's localized morning .

& I Wrote

"The stars press out the subconscious."
A soldier in Desert Storm

1.

And I wrote,
heeding among the nations of the world,
to their coolness (or)
their warmth of spirit .

& I wrote, I
listening to the daily
conversation of men and women in the street

& in the park where,
late at night,
O! only the alligators
stirring now and then

and those who lurk
with reptilian mentality .

Thus, when the moment
seems for all things right

& the grass ——
O! it smells wonderful
under the stars after a rain,

I hear (them) above me
elaborately saying what
we cannot even dream :

2.

le lit inoccupé

A YELP IN THE IDEAL

Song

My teeth are falling out ____
one and then another.
And the gums, in loose pink slabs,
like an unmarked game of scrabble,
are also removed

until my head is almost empty
and, opening my mouth wide
in the mirror,
I can see
right to the base of my brain, can
see *into* it a little,

see past the white *thrush* in my throat
(a fungus in small patches)
to the hemorrhoid of grey matter
to thought which strains for speech,

finding no words
for its itch and ache and reason

but empty-headed, in-
articulate
song.

The Universe Worm

for Sir Herbert Grierson, editor of
the first definitive edition of John Donne

I.

Feverish,
the city that never sleeps.

It spreads its glow for miles around.

Because of it
we cannot see the stars —

only this patch above us to know
we are part of the universe.

Yet, can you sit still beneath it?
If so, for how long?

witness some comet or the leaf
which drifts with equal brightness
catching the light from your bedroom?

And the trees speak to you here at ear level
for you have climbed to the roof
and are numbered among them.

If all of your life
you have practiced to do this:

sit as an animal
without thought or distraction,

see the great shapes leaping in the upper branches —
you will know how the attention is fixed:

a skewered morsel
tempting the Night

which may pounce,
drawing everything through its black eye.

2.

"Look at it this way," persuaded old Sir Herbert,
"the ra-ahspberry worm is pure

ra-ahspberry. What
harm that you have eaten him
with ra-ahspberries at tea?"

"Good common sense," I reply, and
if true, then

the Universe Worm (that's me!)
is pure starry sky!

Dawn

Rising from the broken knife,
rising from the broken sheath of night,

Rising from the broken air
rising from the Pity Heart of man,
light!

Light!
        the inviolable sheer
        sheath that I slip on

is not unlike
the shield of faith,
the low, loin-swathing girdle of truth,
the breastplate of righteousness
as Tychicus describes it to the Ephesians ——

not unlike
the   "whole armor of God".
(Its link of surreal mail
is not unlike this helix
of young air) .

A Thin Peel of Moon

a thin peel of moon:

But children know the right
and always choose it——

Right??

at a loss,
the little cur

sits down .

Night Fishing

Frantically we
threw them back, fearful

of holding them. In a last and spectacular
effort, they

flipped from our hands, some reaching
the sea, sending up a shower

of phosphorescence, dragging a white
wake, but others spilling

back upon the floor that was paved with them
(for our catch had been tremendous) and

leaping toward the light as mullet
will, toward the light

which shredded the sea and shattered
the night all around, struck

us in the face, the chest, hurled
themselves against our bodies.

In panic then we grabbed at them (though
fearful of electrocution) for

the light all
seemed to come from them, the floor

a mirror of bright fish in which we saw ourselves,
gasped at the sight,

will not forget
that vision.

Later we thought,
hauling in the comrade who had dived beneath the boat

for protection, how
what we should have done was throw ourselves

down, working our way into the bed of fish
for insulation.

But then we strove
for propitiation (needing, we thought, to

rid ourselves of catch
taken beyond some holy and unwritten limit),

threw them back,
threw them all back,

til the boat rode high in the water
and the light, you said,

shielding your face and cursing it,
now came from *me*.

But *I* saw, as you turned,
your black skin glistening

(for the lightning still popped upon the glassy sea
though no thunder ever broke the silence

to warn us of its coming and going—
only the thud of boots

against the gunwale,
the slap of flesh against flesh and, as we

stumbled, the clattering of oarlock and pail),
I saw

the jaw of small flames which,
wreathing you, gnashed white as sharks' teeth

then died, leaving us in darkness,
cursing our stupidity as rain fell.

Considering

Considering . . .
. . . how bees
swim in slight air, makes
that medium seem
heavier to them then than
to me
water .

This one,
clasping
a spikelet of sweetgrass, flails
like a bumbling lover,
spins
on an axle yawing and
too slim
for its
brusque paws and greedy
body, yet
takes what it needs, inseminates some
floral apparatus, then
air-lifts, an
ominous and
sudden
helicopter,
swelling the air with gas fumes.

Gazing at the swaying
monster
through an almost uninhalable
viscosity
of light and
color,

I feel drunk,
awash in the rainbow of
bumblebee exhaust,
considering. . .
. . .how mere
proximity to so much

fullness

distorts
my perception
of things, how
so much

certainty

in matters of exchange
strokes
at the quick of existence.

As for the grass,
its pollination thus achieved, the slight
bowed rod released springs back,

leaps

free
and
nimble
as yet
unaffected by this
intercourse
with its burly
lover who

treading air above it
one moment still
(the nectared cargo sloshing
in its
underbelly almost
perceptible
through the black and
glistening shell),

revs his motor, then
slips into gear
and

zooms away.

relinquishing
my senses which,

shaking free of one another, now
apprehend the world each

singly,

as it is

before love
wastes us
with its

no gainsaying and
unimpeachable

flame .

The Feast

Round
the end of the beach where
wind had dropped and
the world was plasma
colorless and
still —

only
the scavenger gull,
only the day-moon spreading and
spreading her nets, dragging
the channels of the ear for her crop
of music

and
the night hawk
strafed all flash
that signaled flesh to its
keen eye —

a half-
buried oil drum gave
to my touch
response
without apology or hesitation

so that
I
first
leapt back
like a dog licking blood,
scanning and ascertaining the compass
of my solitude

then fell to,
unleashing a
ready and thundering
rhythm, tapping some deep
source in the
rusty barrel

until my
hands, my
arms, my savage
face were
red with this music which

spilled forth,
tinging all that
sea and
sky, gory
aethereal.

The Island Rabbi

1.

You can read, Rabbi,
Like an enchanted man ———

Why do you hesitate and look behind you?
Why cling to the tree?

Why are you dressed like a caterpillar
in old green overalls?

Rabbi! Rabbi!
Which letter is first?
Which last?
Which next to last?

2.

"To seek for it," he said,
"the Ineff . . . ———"
He was silenced by the scolding of a bird.

Dangling from threads,
some inch worms:

a gymnast alphabet
performs an unutterable word.

3.

As camphor berries on the tongue
cause its involuntary
writhing, the Name
drew speech:

praises welling to the lips
in unintelligible language.

As camphor which enters the blood stream
renders the flesh invulnerable
to gnats, mosquitoes, flies,

the Name,
coursing throught the Rabbi of the Islands,

renders him oblivious
to mockery and scornful eyes.

4.

Phylacteries: the harness of the mind
(wing-shaped pieces of sea-glass, "the Scriptures")
strapped against his forehead with a crabline.

His fringed shawl
is a tattered net
to cover his *davening* head.

The prayer of kittens in tall grass
comes easily:

he calls them. But . . . .
which is which?
There ought to be seven!
He's missing two! O, sacred confusion
of the numbers! How will he answer to G-d?

"Calm down," says G-d.
"If no other *schule* has summoned you
but marsh, its shoals and schools
of little fishes,
in this *schule* shall you serve."

At low tide, an eternal view! At high,
a spectacle eroded by the sea.

(The Rabbi's eyeglasses
are eroded by his weeping.)

5.

As Moses snoozing in the reeds,
the Rabbi now lies down in them,
a great, long-legged shore bird in his nest.

The loon, alarmed, laughs once, then rests.
The flounder in its quilt of mud is sleeping.

Out of the wind and safe (here,
where those sacred passages have led him),

still waters mirror a red sky:
his cup runneth over.

G-d's Law

The Hassidim: I love them so much!
They've got G-d's Law copied in their hearts.

"In mine," he said,
"there is the western end of a Carolina island

where, tiny in the distance,

black within the red world of evening,
two

companionable mongrels
reflect

upon the stilts
of their shadow legs."

Revelation

The red sun of dusk
The red sun of dawn ———

He stood between them .

And a voice cried out,
Who sees dawn and dusk at one moment
Must die!

He turned then,
Denying dawn, like Peter,

Chose dusk,
The hour before dark,
Chose the Western sky .

Yet knew he had seen some *fact*,
Blundered onto some rare
Stage of love, naked and forbidden .

Wondered what *kind* of death?
Wondered *how* that flagrant,
Leaping Lord would kill him?

Epic

At first
the story swept along .

Breaking
from some tumescence

line after line
fell upon the page .

Then,
running slowly,
out of the gold junction,

(a more) complicated
(*Truth*)

And I was lying on my side,
my life half over,
mouthing,

"Ooh, aah, ou, ee, aie!"

Standstill

"What shall we do?"

The streets and boardwalk were all crowded,
People milling————

It had come to a standstill
and the question was,
"What shall we do?"

And I cried, "Look at the sunset"
craning my neck this way and this

to glimpse it
through the shifting
interstices of people .

We Were Going to March

We were going to march against
high possibles, animal
experiment, the
suicide, could
we do this? And the
rodent we kept in a steel cage
had grown
and we felt, we thought, that … *cheese?*
that scratching behind the ears will
produce an ecstasy and
the refrigerator is
to blame, *we* understand,
but he got out,
voracious, thick
like a fur bomb
and I was one of them I
tried not to think.

It was the verge of twilight
when the senses wake
and I stood upon the building's
crumbling ledge
looking west across the city
like my mother in her long, black gown,
nothing in her long, black hair,
where the sky was streaked with red.

And there is nothing we can do about it.

To the north, there, on the forest's edge,
a birch had fallen and gleamed whitely.

Beauty, Beauty

Beauty, beauty, skin deep
and the thing is opened up before our eyes:

beneath the surface, *life*:
killing in the usual manner

and the spider, the revisionist spider
is sent out to snare hearts.

By the light of her revision,
we see History: behind

the potted palms and gay night-life of that famous place
where She wobbles toward us like a bride,

cooks dress meat:
greedy little horses daubed in flour
even as they chomp,
corn husks bristling from active lips.
And the poet has *so* much to say!

How one wants to clean the mind!
If only before death we could clean out our thoughts!
But for that, God would have to seize us
and scrape out our brains,
drawing our discomfort with them.

—What *are* your plans?
—I'm going to try with my little bit of money—
God knows what.

—Do you want to go to Death?

—No! It can't be answered in that way, here,
at night, where the lights burn all night long!
What's wrong with you, *con*? Qu'est-ce que tu veux?
O, God! It boils down to too much!

But at dawn, in some truck stop on the edge of town,
the coffee maker, reaching its culmination
in a soft gasp of steam, sighs

"*HOLY*"

In That Day

In that day, he which shall be upon the housetop, and his stuff in the house, let him not come to take it away; and he that is in the field, let him likewise not return back. Remember Lot's wife. Whomsoever shall seek to save his life shall lose it; and whomsoever shall lose his life, shall preserve it. –Luke 18:32–33.

Leaving everything,
we run.

The forest is ablaze.
And the wind, which springs up suddenly,
preceding the sou'wester,
blows smoke ahead of us, darkening the sky.

I knew the forest burned—*some*where.
Considered leisurely, what *would* I save?
Well, certainly the dog's leash—
that we not be parted
          in the pandemonium of spreading flame—
   and my poems.

But suddenly,
the lights die in my cabin, as smoke streams round
and the dog, tearing in from his far forest roamings,
the beautiful bright hound
          who has outstripped the fire's frontier,
                                        circles once wildly

that I submit me to his domain
where the sound of the running brook questions
so sweetly the heart—

And I linger in that day
as smoke flows past and the wind rips at my hair,

unable to remember where, in the rooms behind me,
the braided thong and pages are—
some here, some there, held together with paper clips...

Then,
abandoning my art and animal connection
as a creature its young to the flames,
I follow the text that must teach me,
"Turn not back!"

And, remembering Lot's wife,
I race!

Doggerel

"Come on!" I said,
as the dog sank down into the grass.
"It's time we were getting in."

"No," she said.
"I need to meditate on Nature,
the beauty of this Nature,
of this twilight,
the twilight of our Iives,
our animal lives,
the short-lived beauty of our lives
which occur in Nature.
How else may we understand our nature,
our animal nature, mortality and beauty
and the opportunity to contemplate them
that life gives?"

She was only seven,
but the fur around her ears and muzzle was already grey.

"Alright," I said,
squatting down beside her
as some hungry god or goddess stuck his fork into the sun
which bled out like an egg yolk behind the hill
while Venus became visible
and I thought, as I always do,
how as the morning star, she's Luci-
fer, Light-bearer (as coni*fer* bears cones
and Jennifer and Christopher bear John and Christ) —

That Venus, in her double role,
should be the rebel archangel
just made me thrill!

And all the while,
the dog sat very still.

Then Jupiter rose in the East,
a forty carat diamond, blue,
while I reviewed the origins (I always do)
of that compound Latin word,

for the old gods
just change their names,
(requiring of us always sacrifice and praise)
the lazily-lipped consonants disguised as new :

thus Ju-piter (Greek, Zeus,
from the Indo-European *diew*,
the bright, the shining one, the (in French) *dieu*,
is *dieu-pater* or God-the-Father, He, who
once as Zeus, deposed *his* father, Cronus,
whence *chron*ology); thus,
though I've trouble with the rhyme,
The Eternal banished Time!

And all the while
the dog sat quietly beside me,
encouraging a purer contemplation

as The Dipper became visible,
that perfect astral clock,
circling the fixed pole of our sky, ’til

I ceased to rummage
through the luggage of my language
and my mind became like hers,

quite still.

Surrender

Surrender————

But not in the same manner?
Yes, always in that manner

"Only the hero is . . ." he says,
(only surrender
will liberate his people from endless war

and so he lays his laurels down,
beautiful, strip-naked as a god).

That is one of the trees I have enclosed in a halo———
There are very few in this life.

Black

Some things are really black ——
for instance, coal ——

Have you ever seen coal crushed?
fwhew!
or coal *crush*?

A *wall* of coal I saw fall
on tiny quarrymen,

saw one by one
the dislodging plunge
of massive satin crystals,
saw

        the potential.

Life

"They make a fine young wine
in this part of the country,

(blending)
the two long-kissing *blancs*
with the terror-willing grapes,"

he cried,
ripping off his clothes
as if life were golden .

And it is .

And for the Homeless

And for the homeless,
                                        matchlight,

                                the memorial
        bath

        tub .

May echos out of luck survive this (   )

(the silence is tweaked)

:O, darling, help me .

The Valiant

A white horse zooms across a field .

Behind him, an old house with a long porch
and eaves like a low hat

And the year is the Year of the Horse
And his sign is The Valiant .

Remembering my grannymother,
her last words,

"Go often into the small town
and get drunk" .

It consoled her quite deeply
to have someone think she was

A horse .

Queen

for Rhoda

They'd threatened Queen,
my fancy little mare,
to curb her wild ways.

The sensitive mouth I was
so proud of—
hands light as air—
they'd cut to bleeding.

The horse breakers were blunt—
That would teach her!

So we went side by side as two girl friends
to console ourselves with peppermints
at the county fair.

I held them on my palm like sugar lumps.
She loved them!
Could peppermint anesthetize that glossy violet?
I don't know.

We talked,
picking our way through the crowd,
Queen swishing her tail,
batting her tremendous lashes.

*c.*1980

For Joy

She set out in the world with her favourite thing :
a bucket
to water the tethered horses
which were filthy, thirsty

and some
clasped by the breast
to the May-sty
who were lonely .

The little mares and stallions
were filled with gratitude .

They pawed the dust .
they tried to express it in writing .
They tried to express it beyond their scope of expression :

"Just let me kiss her
in her sequined raincoat and beret !"

The formal juice of the leaves
falls firmly from a packed, unlettered mouth
(i.e., they slobbered on her sleeve) .

The Song

The first note was unreachable, almost. Years
since he'd heard it. Now once again,

appeasing his tuneless croak,
her high sweet whisper struck out easily, ran through
the song like wind through long grass on the Balkan plains.

"You have no time to linger anymore," it says,
"with your oils and perfume. Now,

for all our human sorrow, one panacea:
dawn on the steppes, paired buds
of the horsechestnut, standing alone."

Now she had begun, unceremonious, without
accompaniment, not giving him a chance

to introduce her, to prepare a second generation
for that song, advise them to sit up and take notice,

he dared not stop her, dared not take down
the balalaika or guitar and offer them to her

(though he craved her small white tapered fingers
plucking the strings)

for fear she would break off,
capricious, punitive as she'd begun,

condemn them to a slack, grey evening,
condemn his children to their ignorance
of those mind-glittering elements...

And so, though she ran through it far too quickly,
withholding the emotion from her tone
                                        as though to torture him,

and though the children had withdrawn into their corner
of the single room, united against him,
          deriding his old world ways,

he sat hunched and,
tolerant of anything but that the song be interrupted,
endured the hurried version, indifference, scorn;

anything but that the heritage be untransmitted,
but that The Song, begun again at last now

by this voice uniquely suited to it,
should go unsung.

Voice of Angel

Voice of angel,
voice of dove,

music
restorative.

Voice of blackbird,
voice of crow,

say,
"No."

Hear each bird call
and hear it well.

It tells of heaven
or of hell.

The morning breaks as angel call
encircles all.

In sweet cortège the mourning dove
across the summer lawn doth move,

its grey the fellow of grey dawn
while yet the sun is ripening,

and lapis bunting in their train
do peck the shining ground for grain

as sky of rosy hue
grows blue.

The riddle bird that tells its name
sings next from nest that knows no shame

though close to ground
where fox and vixen do abound.

Then other birds begin to sing,
the blackest bird of scarlet wing

and thrush and wren,
mocker and lark
(*Alaudidae*) that breaks the heart!

But, as within one song contained,
the voice of angel is sustained.

Voice of angel,
voice of dove,

recall to us
the things we love.

Voice of blackbird,
voice of crow,

make known to us
what we must know.

This morning, I,
within my net,
look up at leaf in silhouette,

as black as jet
against a silver sky,
see small birds flying
back and forth

with worm or seed
for hungry mouth,

and I rise, too,
the ground still wet with dew.

And so, throughout the busy day,
the noisy birds keep harmony

'til even-fall
(still sleeps the owl),

dove folds her wing
and no birds sing.

Then angel call
encircles all.

c. 1973

The Tree

The tree
is a signet

cut into the lapis
of my eye

Your face branded
"tree"

and all that I see
I stamp my vision on
as an emblem .

As for
"the inner vision"

(images inherent in the brain
that you call 'poetry')

its essence
is

the extensive, bee-stenciled
brain gasoline .

The Book

You are trying to write a book
but the going's slow and you're bored.

You must change your attitude,
you tell yourself, and
(O! little miracle!) it changes!

You find yourself at this point
opening a book you do not know
with clean, clean hands.

As you turn the pages of which you are innocent,
they cry, "I must fall in love with you !"

Now they are elm leaves,
pressed to the third eye——

This is the book:
veins,
preparations for light and dark,
the cool, green
poultice .

The C Monster In Spring

The composition, *Spring*,
almost exclusively for the treble
(played by the composer himself),
requires, for one note in the bass,
an accompanyist from the audience.

The child chosen last night
threw herself into the role of the "C Monster"
with perfect conviction,
pouncing on the low note with so much stealth and vigor,
that the composer's long, arthritic fingers
wandering like a love-lorn youth
                    along the beach toward middle C
(clearly the dividing line between the land and water),

                    leapt back
as the keyboard was actually splashed,
dissolving the audience in laughter.

Truce

All I remember of the dream
are your two shoes—
the long satin, midnight blue,
gold embroidered slippers that
I bought you to replace the pink
ballet shoes you had ruined
running through the marsh.

Who are you,
young matron of perfect decorum
whom I now hardly know
but once snatched from society's titters
as you tripped on your feet in a dance-athon?
And why have you come into my dream?

Here, in this old southern city,
where traffic turns and daylight blazes
like an army's sabres, cutting off
my mind from its deep source,

and flower women, rising from
the old post-office steps,
rush toward you, thrusting torches
of wild marigold and swamp-glade glads
into your expressionless, pure face,

I wait for you, the motor idling, in my dark car,
to mail your letters and come slipping down the steps,
the dream shoes, which do not go with your street suit,
accentuating your long feet———
which leads me to suspect you are . . .

a *poem* . . . of unusual measure,

the *spondee*,
or libation, spilled in solemn promise
as you slide into the seat beside me and I shift
into low gear, enter the stream of traffic and,
flowing with it through the city, pour slowly out
across the causeways and longbridges
spanning the wide marsh,
into the evening twilight,
back

into the sea from whence,
on those blue toe-shoes,
you originally stemmed,

O, Poem,
O, Ratification.

But Now

"I am
at the lips before speech, at life's
labia,...
her cunt. . ."
(and)
"they
'want to have little beds, and tables
and everything else.' "

from As In The Old Days, *Robert Duncan*

We found ourselves in furniture infested seas
which spoke with the voice of our mother,
swollen with sobs.

"Wherefore, *no*?" she wailed as one betrayed,
while tables nosed us,
and we struggled to escape
the grinning, malevolent appliances
and hopeful chairs.

How was it possible?
We *had* been at Life's labia, her cunt!
But nothing is worth saving now,
time only to dive into her cleavage
as the grey sea rises up,

balancing upon her towering, wild breasts
those two huge cushions of the sofa-bed.

Epitaph

Lies, Beauty

, Snow & Ruin——

Was This

My Life ?

Day Clean *

This hour of cleanliness,
there rises up a force:

the demi-urge
invading with his power___

and I rest
in the implications of my half-sleep
as if, like Job,
I had nothing else to rely on.

The bird dog has it,
with single-minded intention,
holding his point as the covey wavers across the field,

and I, the intensity fading,
might hold it day-long if I tried.

I dreamed last night I'd married — again.
That at the sacrament I have ignored the bread
but swilled the blood in blue, misshapen glasses
like cheap wine.

I have heard my father talking about doubt.
I have heard him, in awe of feminine beauty,
thinking about things:
how whatever else may be— or maybe *not*,
that Mary, Mother of God,
must have the most beautiful skin!

What a beautiful morning!
What beautiful purpose and meaning!
How fresh and dark the kitchen to one bolting coffee,
his fishing gear beside him, before the day's begun:

this hour of cleanliness,
trout rising to the surface:

this power, this emptiness,
this love-affair.

* *South Carolina island expression for that moment before sunrise when the sky is pale but colorless*

Ah!

Running slowly out of the gold junction. . .

Ah! may have even caught the (pure
thought at its source)
by going feintly in

as through the valley, in the shadow of my death,
I lightly tread,

(for) I'm honored, *honored*
to have been sired,

to grow subtler and subtler,
slip at last past one's own dogs,
to catch History with the right eye while smiling.

First I went into the cold wild monstrous,
spent one hundred thousand days there in perplexity

and in the valley, in the deep valley,
cautiously unanxious I became

for it's *good* to keep in touch and yet,
you can make this little mac *go* somewhere!

Great! the colors are all shaky,
they're pure in bare fingers
and we leak the linament, the linament of light

as sun breaks through
and in that light,
though we don't say this, for our parents
taught us nothing and we get drunk,
you might just remember
what a good time we had.

Oh! It's like Christmas! It's so sexy, so exciting!
the tree line seen against a flash of lightning
through a veil of falling snow

but if you ask (the blond woman)
how she feels, she grasps her throat, her heart,
her abdomen, her loins, "It's everywhere, it's everywhere,
and there's nothing you can do about it."

—The corpses of three white dogs
What shall I do with them?

—Nothing. Let them die, let them rot.
From the fang of the dead dog
like serum from a hypodermic,
a new sun arises,
like sap culminating in a golden fruit .

Ah! They're complex systems of pure gold,
I see them,
painted in pure dawn,

the air wild with birds unsettled from their roosts,
the bough heavy with ripe fruit .

And if, at evening,
neither joy nor grief prevaileth,

the mind is clear,
the silences are golden,
(birds dart through bushes spangled with red berries),
And now she runs at a golden pace.

And, glancing at midnight,
through open windows into the hall,

sees in the dance
and in the form of the dance

things she understands
and things she does not understand

and wonders.

Poem In Five Verses

for George Seferis

1.

And when it reached the scalding point,
it surged forth,

broke through my weak clay side
and fled to you

as though this ocean were
your animal, your white hound.

Thus I learned how images come into being,
how the eyes are rained out windows
of some high ruin .

And the heart is a mold
that when broken
releases its impression
which stands as an inner reality.

2.

Thoughts not easily formulated:
these are the true ideas.

The mind
is a room

where clothes are being sorted,
sweaters and old coats
piled on the beds,

and the only real thought
is the one they will chase out:

the moth
    who opens her wings
like the covers of a rare edition.

3.

So (it seems) the greatest
calamity

is to succeed
without really trying .

                    For then,
no sacrifice ————no
broken heart
    relinquishing
        some depth of vision————

The lamb we fattened?
We kept him as a pet

and missed the full
tragedy of our lives.

4.

In a trickle at first, the tragic sense:
starlight filling the eyes .

Farther and farther I look until blind—
the star flooded sight, the desert cry of night vision!

I set my foot beside his on the road,
trot along like a child—
in insufficient measures.

Yet, emulating him, Seferis—
I see the past, see years ahead of me,
and take, amid circumstance, a stance.

5. Invoice

Raising his eyes to the window above the stove,
he caught the reflection—

the White Bird in Appearance, the
lofty, gliding soul.

He turned then,
relinquishing that vision,

The Illusion Book,
its margin of silver water along the shore—

turned on an axis,
turned round the dreaded
deformation long
hidden there, found

nothing,
a simple, empty core.

Rising from the marsh at his approach,
white birds
present their bills
(ah! what he owes them!)

That blue line,
he thinks (toeing the old tackle),

in the margin of this ledger,
a triangular lead weight attached

to leash the sea .

UNCOLLECTED POEMS

We Leap From A Trap

We leap from a trap
and scatter through the hills,
an over-laden trap of dogs

It is night and and strangely night

no talent –   –
It is all love

was my grandfather's mother's father's moth

Hail, Mary! full of grace!
The Lord is with thee!

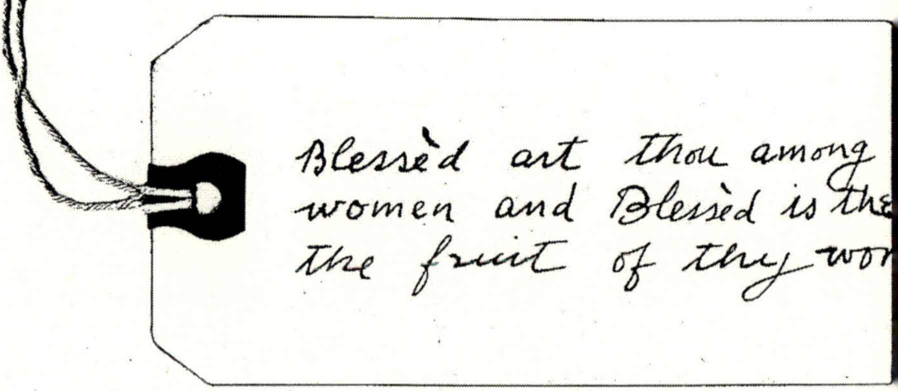

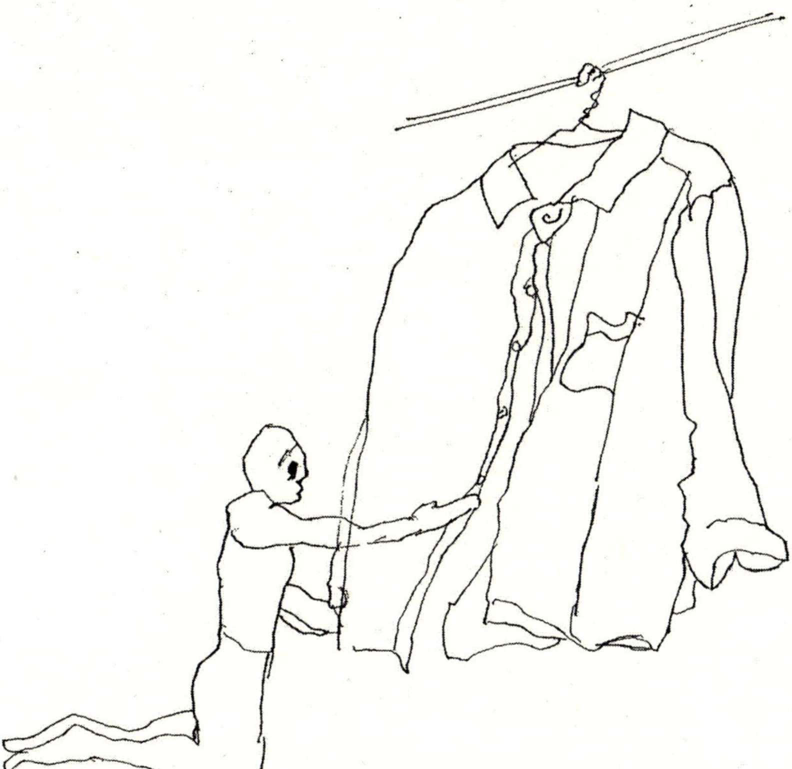

y, full of Grace, the Lord is wi

among women
& blessed   is thesweep of thy sword

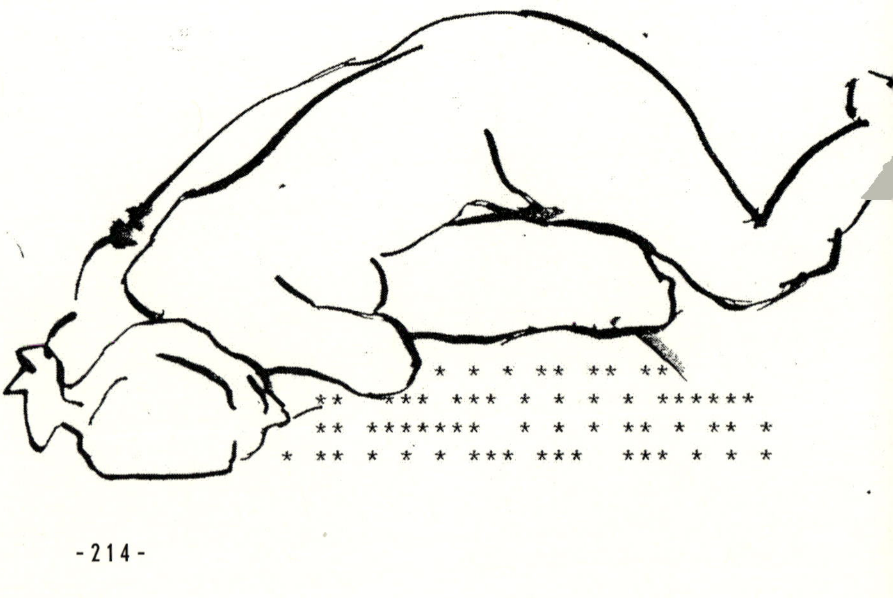

* * * ** ** **
** *** *** * * * * ******
** ******* * * * ** * ** *
* ** * * * *** *** *** * * *

and blessed is the root of Thy name.
Holy Mother of God,
pray for us sinners ,

and at the hour of our death.

Holy Mary,
Mother of God,
pray for us

now and at the
hour of our

❖

Our little boat?
I can see it __
I can draw it in three sizes:

the little,
the tiny little,
the tiny, tiny ···

But memory grows painful
as the white mare staggers to the water's edge___

And you are old, stalwart,
stock-market analysts.

(At the hour of our death)
we should ask three things___ :

I don't know what the third one is
but the first are

Grace and Pardon.